CONTEMPLATIVE
VISION
PHOTOGRAPHY
AS A SPIRITUAL PRACTICE

CONTEMPLATIVE
VISION
PHOTOGRAPHY
AS A SPIRITUAL PRACTICE

DIRK DEVRIES

CHURCH
PUBLISHING
INCORPORATED

To my husband Tim,
who believes in me even when I don't,
and to our cat-boys, Romeo and Willy,
who teach me how to live in the holy now.

_____

Church Publishing
19 East 34th Street
New York, NY 10016
www.churchpublishing.org

Cover art by Dirk deVries
Cover design by Marc Whitaker, MTWdesign
Typeset by Rose Design

A record of this book is available from the Library of Congress.

ISBN-13: 978-1-64065-134-0 (pbk.)
ISBN-13: 978-1-64065-135-7 (ebook)

CONTENTS

PART 4: RESOURCES // 133

PART 1

CULTIVATING CONTEMPLATIVE VISION

CHAPTER 1

A NEW ROLE FOR PHOTOGRAPHY

Photography provides an exceptional opportunity to experience being fully alive in the present and attuned to my surroundings.[1]

—*Phillippe L. Gross and S. I. Shapiro*

The Many Uses of Photography

Today, it seems, we have all become photographers. Not only are quality cameras inexpensive, the advent of digital photography has made photography accessible to all, without the expense that once came with purchasing film and then paying for developing and printing. The continuing evolution of the smart phone, capable of taking and instantly sharing high resolution photos (not to mention the ability to manipulate these photos using a variety of intuitive phone apps) puts the possibility of quality photography into the hands of millions who otherwise wouldn't invest in an actual camera. Include the many ways we now share photos—Instagram, Pinterest, Facebook, Twitter, Flickr, Google Photos, Photobucket, Snapfish, etc.—and it becomes clear photography is a part of our lives in a way unprecedented in history. As I said, we are all photographers.

But we use photography in different ways, serving a variety of purposes.

Photography Preserves

With our pictures, we document our lives, help ourselves remember, capture, and preserve our stories. With photography, we freeze moments, hoping, at a later point, to relive what has

---

1. Philippe L. Gross and S. I. Shapiro, *The Tao of Photography: Seeing Beyond Seeing* (Berkeley, CA: Ten Speed Press, 2001), 5.

passed, to return and feel again the warmth or wonder, happiness or triumph. You undoubtedly treasure photos of your family celebrating past Christmases and birthdays, photos documenting trips to the beach or the mountains, the Grand Canyon and Disneyland, photos preserving baptisms, graduations, and marriages. Look back through your photo albums (printed or digital)—your past lives here.

Photography Reveals

We also use photography to expose and combat injustice, to reveal what others try to hide, and, by revealing, to help, to serve, to save. Think back to the times your eyes have been opened—and your heart torn—by images of suffering, and you've responded, "No, this must not happen." I recall the horrifying Holocaust pictures I was shown as a child. I think of the famous image of the nine-year-old Vietnamese girl (whose name, by the way, is Kim Phúc) burned by napalm, crying in pain, running naked down the road. Most recently we've seen photos of the bodies of Syrian, Afghan, and Burmese refugee children who drowned when their boats capsized. We've looked into the anguished faces of children and parents separated at our southern border. Such photos inform and incense . . . and in many cases force change.

Photography Connects

Photos help us enter and better understand the experience of others, to learn about different cultures, of other ways of being in the world. As a kid, I devoured my parents' issues of *National Geographic*; I learned about Eskimos and aborigines, African tribes and Native Americans, migrants and immigrants. Through the power of photography, I felt the heat, tasted the dust, winced at the pain, cried at the tenderness displayed by parents and children struggling in the far corners of the world, people whose relationships, hopes, and needs were very much like mine. Photography unites us with the world.

Photography Celebrates Beauty and Elicits Wonder

Of course, not all photographs are beautiful, and a good photograph can be intentionally disturbing (as mentioned above), but photography also reminds us of the goodness in the world and God's amazing, boundless creativity. Other than family members and friends, what do you suppose are the most photographed subjects? Objects of beauty: flowers and landscapes, rivers and lakes, towering mountains and crashing waves. Been on social media lately? Scrolling through my Facebook page today, I enjoyed photos of hummingbirds, Colorado mountain passes, a friend's amazing garden blooms, and, of course, cats and kittens . . . *lots* of cats and kittens. Photography brings joy, reminds us that, in spite of the suffering in the world, beauty and goodness, wonder and awe still exist. Photos inspire, encourage, amuse, heal.

But Wait, There's More!

There's something else photography can do for us. Photography also offers a means of meditation and reflection, a method of prayer, a key to open the imagination, a doorway into stillness, depth, and meaning. For those who pursue it, *contemplative* photography invites us to slow down and notice, to heighten awareness, to see the extraordinary in the ordinary. Photography can be a form of contemplation, a spiritual discipline, motivated, not by the desire to *produce* something, but by the desire to *be* something, to be in process, open and present, ready to be refreshed, to receive insight.

Spiritual Practice

If you are reading this, you likely already understand the importance of spiritual practice, and you are now or have been a "spiritual practitioner." What is a spiritual practice? I offer this simple definition:

> *A spiritual practice is an activity in which you engage, intentionally and regularly, with the goal of helping you to connect more deeply with God.*

More broadly, a spiritual practice is an activity with the goal of helping you to connect more deeply with self, others, meaning, the universe, etc. I'm okay with this broader definition too, and, in fact, am comfortable rolling all of this up into my definition above; to connect more deeply, more authentically with self, with others, and with creation, is all a part of connecting more deeply with God.

Spiritual practices abound. Going to church, praying, reading scripture, singing hymns and spiritual songs, taking Holy Communion—all are common forms of spiritual practice. But there are hundreds of others, including those from other religious traditions and those that reach far back into history. A search of the internet (or a library or bookstore, digital or brick-and-mortar) yields many possibilities, from walking a labyrinth to journaling, from coloring mandalas to writing poems.

One form of spiritual practice—meditation—is, for many, their primary spiritual practice. There are many ways to meditate. Fr. Thomas Keating's method of Contemplative Prayer revives an ancient prayer practice which, since the mid-70s, has found acceptance by Christians from many denominations. *Lectio Divina* (Latin for "divine/sacred reading") is similarly an old and established practice; its method of *read, meditate, pray*, and *contemplate* combines the reading of scripture with a response of meditation. Numerous websites offer guided meditation and meditation training, some from a Christian perspective, others from other religious traditions (such as Buddhism and Hinduism), and still others from a general spiritual perspective (check out *Headspace* or *Meditation Oasis*). Again, a search of the internet or your favorite bookseller yields options, both overtly Christian and more broadly "spiritual." What do they share in common? The intention to calm the mind and create "space" for something of meaning to arise, whether an encounter with God, our own essential self, or something in the world around us ready to be noticed. We will uncover additional benefits of meditation as we look more closely at photography as a form of spiritual practice (and, I would say, a form of meditation).

Meditation and Photography

In meditation, we purposefully sit in silence, allowing the mind to clear, the input to cease, the chatter to stop. Doing so creates space, space for something more essential and authentic to emerge. What rises will often be something we have not even been conscious of because it exists at a deeper level.

Meditative (contemplative) photography seeks to do the same, to deliberately engage in a simplified, quiet process that allows space for our creativity to be released without the filter and censor of the mind, without the interference of thought or judgment. As with other art forms, this can usher us into the experience of flow, where time and place recede into the background and we are fully in the moment, fully ourselves, fully engaged with our subject, and fully receptive and responsive to the presence of God and the Holy Spirit.

The links between photography (of the meditative sort) and meditation (of any sort) are numerous, and we'll explore these more fully in the following chapters. For now, keep in mind that photography can, itself, be a form of meditation, as reflected in these terms, which, for me, are roughly synonymous:

- contemplative photography
- meditative photography
- expressive photography
- Zen photography
- soulful photography
- photographic prayer
- engaged photography
- conscious camerawork
- photographic awareness

For Reflection:

1. When and in what ways have you pursued spiritual practice(s)? What came of your spiritual practice(s)?

2. Assuming you enjoy photography as a hobby, to what extent and in what circumstances have you been aware that "something more" is happening, that there is a connection between the taking of pictures and your relationship with God?

3. If you have already experienced this connection, what, through your photography, have you discovered about God? About yourself? About others? About the world around you?

CHAPTER 2

A SPIRITUALITY OF SHUTTING UP (STILLNESS AND SILENCE)

Be still and know that I am God.
—*Psalm 46:10* NRSV

A Spirituality of Shutting Up

Don't just *do* something, *sit* there.

Be still.

Be.

Doing can be a way to run away from ourselves, from others, and from God. Silence and stillness call us to be present . . . fully present . . . in a way we seldom allow. Silence can be difficult, because we know, intuitively, that we may not like what we discover. When God meets us in silence, God brings along reality (*is*, in fact, Reality), without distraction and without escape. We meet our true selves, the good and the bad. If we are willing to embrace reality, it equips us to live fully in the world, without illusion, without self-delusion.

I want to be there, and in meditation as well as in contemplative photography, I can practice this. I'm learning, slowly, to be silent and not be unnerved by it. I have come to believe that God is going to be there, just as always, and that no matter what may surface, it will be okay. *I* will be okay.

You will be okay.

Silence on our part indicates an openness to transformation. The more we think and talk, the less opportunity God has to lead us into new territory. I imagine God just waiting until I stop talking . . . or until my mind stops jumping erratically from topic to topic: What am I making for dinner? Should I check e-mails? My back aches. *Squirrel!*

As the Taoists say, "To the mind that is still, the world surrenders."

And so I encourage a *spirituality of shutting up* . . . in a nice way, of course, and for our own good. I once proposed this title for a workshop: *For God's Sake, Shut Up!* I then amended it to: *For God's Sake (and Yours), Shut Up!*, which seemed less off-putting. The workshop morphed into a series of meditations, and the title was abandoned, but I'm still fond of it. I now use it as a reminder for myself of God's invitation to (as well as the importance of) silence in my life.

The Purpose of Silence

What do we seek in silence?

First, in silence we seek self-knowledge and self-acceptance, to know and nurture ourselves, for, as the saying goes, "only in still water do we see our reflection."

The potential gift in silence is the discovery of our true self, our true identity. At first, in silence, we may experience our restlessness and compulsiveness, our unexpectedly strong desire to produce, to influence, to make an impact. But if we can sit with the silence, both exterior and interior, who we truly are emerges, and we have the opportunity to embrace all our disparate selves, the ones we admire and the ones we fear, the ones we welcome and those we would just as soon keep hidden. Being a complete, integrated (whole as in "holy") person asks us to welcome and integrate all of who we are.

Second, we look for silence to deepen intimacy. You only have as much connection with others as you have with yourself. You experience others as you experience yourself in silence. Do you trust yourself in silence? Do you, as mentioned, welcome and integrate all aspects of yourself? Do you find yourself lovable? Authentic? A source of comfort? If so, then you will also trust others; you will welcome them, warts and all; you will find them as lovable, authentic, and comforting as you find yourself.

Third, in silence we seek to know God. Stillness is the place where God reveals God's self as God-with-us, the God who anchors us, centers us, gives the very self of God to us in unconditional, limitless, unrestrained love.

As we relax into silence, we have a chance to hear the "still, small voice" that Elijah heard on the mountain, after the earthquake, the fire, and the wind subsided. The NRSV tells us that Elijah finally encountered God in "a sound of sheer silence" (1 Kings 19:12). The passage does not say that once things quieted down, Elijah could finally hear the voice of God; no, the passage suggests that this "sheer silence" was itself the presence of God. *Elijah knew God in the silence.*

Is this possible for us? I think the basic premise of Christian meditation is exactly this, to know God in the "sheer silence," with a knowing that moves beyond questions and answers, beyond words, a knowing that strives for nothing but pure presence. Silence invites us to simply *be with* God in a deeper, more profound way.

Silence and Contemplative Vision

We live in a noisy world, a world intent on keeping us from knowing ourselves, knowing others, and knowing God. Its uproar erects a barrier to silence and intimacy, to authentic connection. Such it has always been.

Much of the time, we have no choice but to live with the noise: We commute. We watch the news. We constantly monitor our phones. We watch TV, stream movies and music, attend meetings, and go to movies, plays, and concerts. All of this may be necessary, pleasurable, or both, but all of this also contributes to the noise, distracting us, often crowding out time to attend and listen, to foster awareness and mindfulness.

The noise doesn't have to win. You have a choice to settle into stillness, and this is an important first step in the process of contemplative photography, of gaining contemplative vision. Just as silence opens us to the presence of God in meditation, it opens us to the presence of God observed through the camera lens. It makes us receptive to the time, place, and subject for our photographs, the time and place where we find peace, depth, communion with ourselves and others, and the subject matter in which we see the face of God.

When we set out to take expressive, engaged photos, we start with quiet time, perhaps even a time of meditation. We first reduce the exterior noise as much as possible, taking practical steps like turning off the TV, silencing the cell phone, getting away from others. We then do the same with the interior noise. If you're experienced in meditation, you may already know how to do this. For the rest of us, simple practices like sitting quietly as we observe our breathing—in, out, in, out—will do the trick. My "theme" word at this point in my life is *stillness*, so I will repeat this silently to myself, usually with each exhalation; when my mind wanders, I return to the word—*stillness*. Another option is to continually repeat the verse found at the beginning of this chapter: *Be still and know that I am God.*

Some use the Jesus Prayer, which likely originated with the Desert Mothers and Fathers of the fifth century: "Lord Jesus Christ, Son of God, have mercy on me, a sinner." You can abbreviate this prayer in several ways, from "Jesus Christ, Son of God, have mercy on me," to "Jesus Christ have mercy," to simply "Jesus." In all cases, you follow the breath, say a focus word, or repeat a favorite verse of scripture to help quiet what is sometimes referred to as the "monkey mind," chattering like a monkey in a tree, annoying and distracting, sort of like this:

The Monkey and the Tree

Your thoughts
chatter like a monkey.

You are not the monkey.

You are the magnificent,
stately,

ancient tree,
reaching to the clouds,
rooted in the earth,
offering shade,
silent,
strong,
and wise,
through whose branches
races the monkey.

Shrug your massive branches,
and let the monkey fall to the forest floor.
He is not hurt,
only offended.

For a while, at least,
love the Stillness
you are.

For Reflection:

1. When and where are you able to enter/embrace/welcome silence? How difficult (or easy) is it for you to find/create silent space in your life?

2. What part (if any) has silence played in your photography thus far? Think about your favorite times and places to take pictures.

3. How might you make room for more silence in your life, not only for the sake of photography, but for your life of faith as well?

CHAPTER 3

WELCOME TO THE NOW (PRESENCE AND MINDFULNESS)

Photography provides an exceptional opportunity to experience being fully alive in the present and attuned to my surroundings.[1]

—*Author Unknown*

Flow

On an afternoon early in June, I sit on the cement with my camera in the heart of the Denver Botanic Gardens. Before me sit dozens of plastic pots of dahlias—pink, orange, yellow, white, purple, variegated—all waiting to be planted. I switch out my standard lens for my macro lens and lean in, eye to the viewfinder. The flowers are gorgeous, layer upon layer of petals, spreading out in concentric rings from the center of each bloom. Close-up, each flower becomes its own pure, soft, limitless landscape. Awesome.

I take a series of shots in which each bloom fills the frame. I back off a bit and capture entire flowers, then come in close again so only a quarter or so of each bloom is visible. I change from the viewfinder to the rotating screen on the back of the camera and place the camera below a flower, so I can take pictures upward, with blue sky or green trees blurred in the background, providing contrast to the color of the bloom. I focus in on the underside of a flower, where the stem joins to its back. I return to the viewfinder and capture images with a bloom of one color in the foreground and blooms of other colors as background.

---

1. Philippe L. Gross and S. I. Shapiro, *The Tao of Photography: Seeing Beyond Seeing* (Berkeley, CA: Ten Speed Press, 2001), 5.

I am completely lost in the moment, unaware of time, of people around me, of anything other than the dahlias. I realize, at times, that I'm forgetting to breathe. I take scores of photos, and twenty minutes pass, then thirty, and I am only aware of one thing—the flowers . . . the amazing, intriguing, lovely flowers.

I am in *the flow*.

Do you experience *the flow?* Flow is the merging of an activity with a state of intense, timeless, receptive awareness. In flow, our inner self melds seamlessly with our outer actions. Time passes quickly, even seems to disappear. We focus solely on what is before us, in our hands, emerging from our imagination. Moments of flow are marked by spurts of creativity, and one may feel as if one is either sinking or floating. The release of endorphins leads to intense concentration. Flow brings with it feelings of peace, joy, satisfaction.

All of this characterized my encounter with the dahlias. I love such moments, even though I'm unaware of what's happening until I take a deep, satisfying breath and disengage, moving on to another subject.

Coming into the Now

One significant goal of spiritual practice is to be fully present *now*, in the flow, in this moment, because this moment is really all we have. The past is gone and cannot be retrieved, except through memory, so set aside the past. The future lies ahead, accessible only through speculation, so release the future. Even when one gets to the future, it's no longer the future, but the new now. Now is all that exists. The present is where life happens.

We typically engage in daily activities while our minds dwell, not on what we're doing, but on what happened earlier in the day (or yesterday, a month ago, or years ago), reliving and analyzing, going over what we could have done, should have said. Rehashing the past keeps us locked into the emotions that may have been appropriate then but are irrelevant now. And pity the activity we're in the middle of, like cooking, watering the garden, talking with our spouse or children—we're only half there, half attending, and very likely, not enjoying it much, not feeling the contentment that comes with being fully present.

We engage in daily activities while our minds dwell on worries about the future, stressing over events that probably won't happen, while, once again, short-changing what we engage in *now*.

God lives in the now, in the present moment, eager to meet and walk with you, so why not join God where God can be met? Here. Now.

This we call *mindfulness*, the process of bringing one's attention and focus to what happens in the current moment. Meditation provides one method for developing mindfulness, and the same techniques we discussed in chapter 2 for welcoming inner stillness help in this process. Stillness and silence open the space; mindfulness steps in to occupy it. Once the mind is quiet, it fully opens to all that is available and waiting in the moment.

I learned the power of mindfulness several years ago while receiving therapy to help me better cope with stress. Since I spent an unhealthy amount of time ruminating on both real and imagined hurts, my therapist encouraged me to explore and try mindfulness meditation. So I did: I read about mindfulness, practiced mindfulness, and benefited from mindfulness. I learned to bring my attention into the present moment, to focus on my current activity, and thus to still the endless jabbering of my mind when I couldn't let something go. The clearest example is the simple act of ironing clothes, which I used to find wearisome. I ironed because I had to, not because I enjoyed it, and ironing, unfortunately, offered plenty of time to rethink and overthink, robbing me of contentment.

Then I brought mindfulness to ironing. When I tell people this, I learn two things: first, very few people enjoy ironing, and second, because very few people enjoy ironing, they have a hard time accepting the idea that mindful ironing can bring peace and pleasure. It can. Now when I iron, I am present to the ironing. I feel the distinctive, varied textures of the fabrics as well as the heft and glide of the iron. I observe the variety of colors—blues, greens, browns, grays—and the different patterns—plaids, checks, stripes. I watch steam rise and hear the gurgling and hissing of water in the iron, as well as the creak of the ironing board. I smell the warmed fabric, the scent of detergent and fabric softener. I enjoy with satisfaction the transformation I create, making the rough places plain and the crooked straight (to borrow from Luke 3).

If you're skeptical, I understand, but I assure you, as I am mindful to the ironing, I experience a deep sense of contentment. I am fully with it, in it, present to it, present to the moment. And because I am present, God is also present. Yes, I experience the presence of God in the act of ironing our clothes.

The point is this: learn to do any task mindfully (even those you currently find most burdensome) and you will experience the same freedom and contentment. No, really, you will. That's the power of the present, the now, where God is and you, most definitely, could be.

Nothing is more precious than being in the present moment fully alive and aware.[2]

—Thích Nhất Hạnh

2. Thích Nhất Hạnh, *The Heart of the Buddha's Teaching* (Berkeley, CA: Parallax Press, 1998), 70.

Mindfulness and Contemplative Photography

Contemplative vision requires, then, not only stillness (as we saw in chapter 2), but also mindfulness. Photography offers an ideal activity for the practice of mindfulness, since photography connects you with what is here, now, right in front of you. As our opening quote asserts, "Photography provides an exceptional opportunity to experience being fully alive in the present and attuned to my surroundings." Fully alive. Fully present. Fully now.

When I set out to take contemplative, engaged photos, I take the time, once I'm "on location," to center myself, to come into the moment. I sit quietly, breathe deeply, look around, and let myself settle into the space. I often use this simple prayer (which I also recite in walking meditation):

> Spirit of God,
> in this moment,
> present with you,
> help me to *be*.

I pray this repeatedly, inhaling on the first line, exhaling on the second, and so on. (Try praying this a few times right now and feel how you ease into a more comfortable sense of simply being.)

You may already have—and certainly can develop—your own methods for coming into the present, for entering the now, for preparing for flow. It will enhance not only your experience as a contemplative photographer, but also your experience of other life moments. Imagine bringing such mindfulness to game night with your children or grandchildren, to preparing a meal for someone you love, to tackling a household repair, to playing the piano, or writing in your journal.

Be here, now.

There's nowhere else you can be.

For Reflection:

1. On a scale of one to ten, one representing "I rarely live in the present moment" and ten representing "I'm always living in the present moment," where would you fall? Where would you *like* to fall? How do you bring yourself more fully into the moment?

2. Respond to the statement: *God lives in the now.* What does that mean to you? How do *you* meet God in the now?

3. Try engaging mindfully in some activity that you otherwise label a chore (like ironing). Write about your experience.

CHAPTER 4

CONTEMPLATIVE INTENTION (EMPTINESS AND RECEPTIVITY)

Release expectations. Defy assumptions. Unite with the scene to see, not what you want to see, but what's there.[1]

—*Derek Doeffinger*

Receiving, not Taking

Ever noticed the aggressive nature of photographic language? The language of photography runs counter to the spirit of quiet awareness necessary for contemplative vision:

- We go out *armed* with our cameras.
- We participate in photo *shoots*.
- We *take* pictures.
- We *capture* images.

Are we engaged in meditation or is this a crime spree?

I struggle to find alternative terminology; whatever I come up with sounds clunky in everyday use. But even if we don't change how we speak about photography, we can occasionally remind ourselves that, wherever we go to take pictures, we are guests in the world. Our subjects come to us as gifts, to be honored and respected, not commandeered. We don't *capture* the images, we *receive* them. We don't *take* the pictures, we *welcome* them. For me, the language of receiving and welcoming better reflects our process.

And to receive, to welcome, we must be *silent* and *still* (as we explored in chapter 2), and we must come into the *present*,

---

1. Derek Doeffinger, *The Kodak Workshop Series: The Art of Seeing* (New York: Kodak, 1992), 76.

the *now* (as we explored in chapter 3). To these two require-ments for contemplative vision, we now add a third: we must also be *open* and *receptive*.

Being Open

Photographer Kathryn Marx suggests:

> You've already thought about your subject and know the rea-son why you've placed yourself in a particular situation. But once you are there, you must try to empty your mind of all thought in order for you to be completely in the moment and receptive to your intuition and your surroundings. Simply react to them with uncluttered clarity.[2]

It happens most easily when we stop thinking about what we *ought* to photograph (that historic building, those people, that range of mountains, that flower) and simply immerse ourselves in our surroundings. We can begin by sitting (or standing) in silence. Be open. Breathe. If you wait quietly and patiently, some-thing nearby will call to you: "Psst! Over here. How about me?" When I am in a contemplative photographic mood, I find it bet-ter not to leave the house with a particular expectation of what I might encounter with my camera. I go ready to receive whatever presents itself. And I know when I'm feeling frustrated—"I'm just not getting what I envisioned"—that it's once again time to empty and open the door to inspiration.

I recently spent a week at a conference center in the moun-tains of North Carolina. Opportunities to photograph the lake, the trees, the geese abounded, and I did "receive" quite a few lovely photos of such things, which were to be expected, but my most interesting photos were of objects and places that tapped me on the shoulder when I walked by (or grabbed my ankle), inviting my attention. I offer two examples here, a photo of the

---

2. Kathryn Marx, *Right Brain/Left Brain Photography: The Art and Technique of 70 Modern Masters* (New York: Amphoto, 1994), 114.

gauges on a peeling, abandoned piece of heavy equipment, and wine and water waiting for Holy Communion.

Friends ask, "Did you get some great photos at the conference?" I respond, "Oh, definitely," but when I show them photos like these, they are not what they expect. "I thought you went to some sort of camp . . . you know, with water and woods and stuff?" "Well, yes I did, but these are the things that requested my attention." As I will repeat later, there are extraordinary photos to be discovered in the most ordinary of places.

Openness and receptivity help us to see the extraordinary possibilities. It's as if the photos sometimes take themselves; my contemplative vision takes over.

Emptying

The Greek word *kenosis* means "emptying." The New Testament letter to the Philippians uses the verb form to describe what Jesus did in his Incarnation, "making himself nothing" (NIV) or "self-emptying," depending on the translation (2:7). We generally understand this to mean that Jesus emptied himself of his *own* will to be entirely filled by *God's* will.

Spiritual practice invites us to "empty ourselves" as well. Am I overstating it to say that being a contemplative photographer demands a similar surrender of our will to God's? That depends on how serious we are about pursuing photography as a spiritual practice. Any spiritual practice asks us to empty ourselves to make room for and receive God (or the Spirit, inspiration, wisdom, beauty, truth, meaning). Why not meditative photography as well?

Kenosis, then, can be our "contemplative intention" when we set out in search of meditative photos. I drive, I walk with contemplative intention. I arrive, I sit with contemplative intention. I inhale, I exhale with contemplative intention. I look, I listen with contemplative intention. God honors the intention; the world opens to us as we open to it.

Striving for silence, coming into the present, emptying ourselves to be receptive—all contribute to our contemplative vision.

An Emptiness Prayer

I have heard you speak to me
   in the emptiness of a woodland clearing;
   in the expanse of a deserted beach;
   in the smooth, blank surface of Lake Michigan,
      seething with slow, deep swells;
   in the living room on an Advent evening,
      lit only by the colors of the Christmas tree;
   in the vacancy of grief, or a condo made larger
      by the sudden loss of someone I love;
   in the vaulted, echoing expanse of a cathedral,
      massive, watching;
   in the house I'm leaving for the last time,
      stripped bare of all but memory;
   in the quiet of a hospital room

after the body's been taken away,
where only cooling, rumpled sheets remain;
in the emptiness of a heart,
like a clean glass taken from the cupboard,
waiting on the counter . . .

For Reflection:

1. When have you initiated a photographic session intending to take certain types of photos of specific places, people, or objects but instead found yourself called to photograph things completely different and unexpected? What resulted?

2. When it comes to your photography, what can you do to "empty yourself" and foster openness and receptivity?

3. When, in emptiness, have you heard God "speak"? When, "in emptiness," have you been surprised by what has presented itself to you and to your camera?

CHAPTER 5

SEEING AGAIN FOR THE VERY FIRST TIME (ATTENTION AND OBSERVATION)

Attention is the beginning of devotion.[1]

—*Mary Oliver*

Stop, Breathe, Look, Listen . . .

Do you stop to notice? Rain drips from leaves; standing water mirrors buildings above; birds preen on wet railings; a car splashes past on the street; your umbrella collides with a stranger's; a child in boots jumps into a puddle and giggles; one cold raindrop trickles down the back of your neck. To you, is this just another gloomy, rainy day, or do you engage with the rich variety of sights, sounds, and smells crowding your senses? Do you feel bothered by the rain, or are you receiving all these sensual gifts as inward celebration? *Do you notice?*

Contemplative vision invites us to engage the senses and to fully, intentionally observe the world around us. Everything we've explored to this point—entering into silence, coming into the present, becoming open and receptive—prepares us to deeply experience the world around us. Contemplative vision welcomes, embraces, appreciates, and respects the details of God's great creation, the rich variety of sensual input always flooding toward us.

The mystics tell us that we are immersed in God. If so, we have the opportunity to experience God in everything and everywhere.

---

1. Mary Oliver, *Upstream: Selected Essays* (London: Penguin Press, 2016), 8.

This is a goal of contemplative photography, to use the senses to engage with God and God's world. Obviously, the first sense we use in photography is vision. The lens becomes an extension of the eye. When we photograph, we hope the image that results matches what we see in the moment (or will be an extension or enhancement to what we have seen). You probably know the feeling of satisfaction when you view a photo on your computer screen and say to yourself, "Yes, *that's* the experience I had; *that's* how I saw the light, the color; *that's* the feeling." Similarly, you've also looked at pictures you took and thought, "That's not it at all. It was much simpler to my eye . . . or more colorful . . . or more mysterious." In either case, your hope is always that what you see with the eye is what you capture with the camera. (And, in fact, as your skills advance, what you see and what the camera sees converge more often.)

But vision isn't the only sense involved in your photography. Your other senses engage as well. When you take photos of

 spring lilacs, for example, you want to capture the color (purple, pink, white), the delicate shape of the tiny, individual blossoms, the overall shape of each cluster of blossoms, the contrast between the waxy green of the leaves and the colors of the blooms (and perhaps the blue sky beyond), and so on. These are all things you *see*, and what makes it onto the surface of a photographic print. But what else is captured in that photograph? The heady scent of lilacs in full bloom (sense of smell). The sound of the wind rustling the leaves (hearing). The weighty heft of a large cluster of

blossoms, their velvety feel (touch). The final image you create, when viewed by you or others, evokes all of this. Yes, vision is the primary sense you employ as a photographer, but the act of photography—the what, when, where, and how of taking your pictures—is much more than just a visual experience, it's an overall *sensual* experience.

Jump in, feet first. Immerse yourself—with all your senses—in the experience.

Paying attention, then, is critical. Notice. Observe.

The Benefits of Paying Attention

There are several great benefits to paying attention. First, *it opens opportunities for great photos*, photos you will miss if you *don't* pay attention. Imagine standing with a group of tourists before a famous statue. The couple beside you pose their two children in front of the statue, snap a picture with their phone, and move on. You have the sense that nearly every picture they will take of their vacation will be captioned "Here's Harry and Mimi in front of . . ." There's nothing wrong with that; they are documenting their trip, and that's all they want to do.

But you want something more. You come in close and notice the hands of the statue; they look strong, solid, yet the way they hold that carefully carved lily suggests great tenderness as well. You take some pictures, hoping that the feeling of strength coupled with gentleness will come through in the final image. You look up, noticing how the sun is now behind the figure's head. You try a few photos; will that halo effect you see with the eye come through on the image? In your camera monitor, it looks like it does. You walk around to the other side, noticing how in full, direct sun, the statue's curves and angles flatten, but a few steps later, standing so the sun hits the sculpture from the side, the folds of the clothes reveal far more texture and dimension. How did the sculptor make something so hard and unyielding look so soft and flowing? You pay attention, and you see . . . and enjoy . . . and photograph so much more.

Paying attention also *quiets your mind*. This is a lovely side effect, much like (and related to) what you experience when you silence your inner chatter, come into the moment, and/or get to that place of open receptivity. These are all related, and in a moment we will practice and experience this great benefit of paying attention.

And, last but by no means least, paying attention *makes you grateful*; you realize: "This moment is good. I'm okay, and this world I'm observing is pretty amazing. All is complete; nothing is missing."

Every moment is as full as it needs to be.

Practicing Attention

I awaken early on a summer morning. No need to get up yet, so I remove my earplugs (snoring mitigation) and turn my head to the open window, beyond which the eastern sky is just beginning to lighten. I see the dark outlines of the trees against the pinkish blue of the sky. I listen: the old wall clock ticks; the ceiling fan hums; two or three robins, also just waking up, talk to each other; an occasional car passes on our street; beneath it all is the ever-present, dull roar of the city. Eventually, I even hear my own breath, in and out, in and out. I feel cool air from the window flow over the bed. I feel quiet and, yes, grateful. I relax and feel myself slipping back into sleep.

Wherever you are as you read this, if it's possible, close your eyes. Take a few deep breaths, inhaling, exhaling, inhaling, exhaling. Now listen; what do you hear? Take your time, shifting your attention from sound to sound. Do you hear sounds from nature? People talking? Machinery or electronics? Music? Notice how each sound, as you attend to it, comes to the foreground and all others fade into the background.

Now, open your eyes. Let your eyes relax in one spot, somewhere in front of you. Without shifting your gaze, what do you see? You have the capacity to note items in your peripheral vision as well as directly in front of you; what else is in this broader field? Note, as with listening, that when you focus on one object, the others around it fade. Your attention determines your vision.

Close your eyes again and inhale deeply. What do you smell? The remains of lunch? Someone's cologne or perfume? Your own body? Flowers or trees? Your pets? What associations do these smells trigger?

Now shift your attention to what you feel in your body. Do you ache anywhere? Do you feel tired? Relaxed? Anxious? Identify where your body is in contact with the chair or couch on which you sit. Feel the pressure on your rear, your legs, your arms. If your hands still hold this book, how does the book feel? If your hands rest on fabric, does it feel smooth or coarse? warm or cool?

Open your eyes once again, but this time, look around. Let your eyes become an imagined camera lens and start framing possible photos. Photographic possibilities are everywhere, including right here, right now. And, because you've just practiced focused awareness (using all your senses), you are likely seeing opportunities you would otherwise have overlooked had you not, through this exercise, quieted yourself, come into the moment, opened, received, and observed.

This is contemplative vision. This is *your* contemplative vision.

For Reflection:

1. *Stop, breathe, look, listen* . . . provides a helpful mantra, not only when out taking pictures, but any time in our day when we find ourselves losing focus, caught up in our own or others' drama. Over the next twenty-four hours, see how this helps when you need to center, come back to yourself, get grounded. Write about this experience here:

2. Record below a single instance of attending and observing. Pick a subject (flower, kitchen item, pet, child, book, chair, tree) and spend five minutes just noting everything your senses tell you of your chosen subject. How does it look? sound? smell? feel?

3. Look through a selection of your photographs. Which are most evocative of senses other than vision? Which can you almost "hear" (like crashing waves)? Almost "touch" (like the petals of a rose)? Almost "taste" (like a slice of lemon)? Almost "smell" (like a pine tree)?

CHAPTER 6

HONORING YOUR PERCEPTION (YOUR EXPERIENCE IS YOUR EXPERIENCE)

The photographer projects himself into everything he sees, identifying himself with everything in order to know it and to feel it better.[1]

—*Minor White*

Embrace the Experience as It Is

When we first observe/experience something—discover a striking flower, taste a delicious plate of food, hear an amazing piece of music—the experience is direct, raw, and unfiltered, but almost immediately we start to analyze, burying the experience beneath thoughts and words. The immediate and authentic experience dulls as we evaluate and categorize. We lose the vividness of the unmediated experience.

It may go something like this: Someone I love hands me a freshly baked, warm-from-the-oven, chocolate-chip cookie and a glass of cold milk. This moment feels great—warm, cozy, loving. I take a bite; the gooey chips ooze decadently in my mouth. I close my eyes and say "Mmmm . . ." I take a contrasting sip of chilled milk. Heaven. And then my mind kicks in: *How many calories in this cookie? Could I have another without guilt? Probably lots of fat in these, but how much is saturated? I will have to add ten minutes to my run after this. Is this skim milk or 2 percent? Good thing I'm not lactose intolerant. Wait, are these nuts? Good thing I'm not allergic to nuts. Oh, I'd better say thank you . . . and then I'll ask for another. These are better than the ones my mom makes; I won't tell her that. Blah, blah, blah . . .*

---

1. Susan Sontag, *On Photography: Seeing Beyond Seeing* (New York: Doubleday, 1989), 116.

And the experience of the cookie, if not entirely lost, is certainly diminished. What if I'd simply stayed with the warm, gooey goodness of the cookie and the delightful coolness of the milk? Many experiences need not be anything more than the experience. Analyzing, classifying, arranging, understanding, categorizing, structuring—does this add anything? More often than not, no; in most cases, the experience is complete in itself. In fact, conceptualizing can pull us out of and away from the pure experience.

You can be transformed by creating (or contemplating) a photographic image (or any work of art, including music, dance, poetry), and it can happen without resorting to linguistic, logical processing. It will "make sense" and move you at levels that transcend thought.

As the great French Impressionist painter Claude Monet tells us, "To see we must forget the name of the things we are looking at."[2] In other words, contemplative vision sees for seeing's sake, without labeling. Let the experience of seeing be the experience of seeing. And if, at some point, you want to deconstruct that experience, dissect and disassemble, go ahead, but do so knowing what you're doing . . . distancing yourself from the original, pure experience.

Photography and Feelings

Earlier I observed that, in meditative photography, the pictures often seem to take themselves. The subject makes itself known to you, invites you. You remain silent—inside and out—and your subject says, "Over here. See me. Experience me."

As you take pictures, think less about what you're doing (though always pay attention to where you're walking), nudge the ego out of the way (an obstacle to so much of life), and photograph without the control of the rational mind.

What engages you? Moves you? Go with it.

---

2. Freeman Patterson, *Photography and the Art of Seeing* (Toronto: Key Porter Books, 2004), 10.

This is photography "in the flow," photography that flows; I call it *flowtography*.

Feel your way into it. Respect, embrace, and allow your feelings. The more deeply you feel, the more your photos will reveal. Allow yourself to be moved, and you will enjoy greater rewards as a contemplative photographer. Be penetrable. Be vulnerable. Show yourself.

The more you are moved, the more your images will embody the emotion you are feeling—sadness, contentment, gratitude, wonder, joy, fear, hope. Note that this will include painful emotions as well; though we generally associate meditation and contemplation with positive emotions, like calmness and acceptance, meditation is more about the authenticity of the experience, welcoming and embracing what is real. Photographer Kathryn Marx says, "The greater the range of emotions that you permit yourself to feel and show, the greater is your receptivity to what you see before your viewfinder."[3]

Your Unique Vision and Your Inner Critic

As a photographer (and, indeed, as a human being) you perceive the world in an entirely unique way. No one else shares your singular, contemplative vision. Claim that vision. Own it. Pursue it. Make no apologies for it, especially when others fail to understand or affirm you for it. Take your photos for your sake, not to win accolades from others.

Photograph for God's sake, because you and God engage in this process together. In the taking of photos, you reach for and share the creative power of God. You and God co-create—your lens, God's eye. How empowering is that?

When it comes to your photography (and for that matter, your life), you are probably your own worst critic. To borrow the title of a recent book on creativity, "your inner critic

---

3. Kathryn Marx, *Right Brain/Left Brain Photography: The Art and Technique of 70 Modern Masters* (New York: Amphoto, 1994), 114.

is a big jerk."[4] Your inner critic—internalized from years of being told, "You're not creative," or "Others do that better," or "Who are you to call yourself a photographer?"—loves for you to doubt yourself, to dismiss your gifts and talents, and to replace your contemplative vision with practical, prosaic vision. "Find something worthwhile to do," it says, "and leave the contemplation to *real* mystics. Stop wasting your time. I mean, seriously, what's the point?" Ah, your dear, well-intentioned but ultimately misguided inner critic. It speaks not for your essential self nor for God. It speaks from fear and ignorance, wanting you to stick with safety and certainty. Your inner critic fails to realize that a vibrant, faith-filled life is lived at the edge, at the point of blessed uncertainty and sacred risk.

Sadly, your inner critic does not share your contemplative vision. Acknowledge its presence, thank it for its input, escort it to its room, and close and latch the door. It will escape from time to time. When that happens, be loving, but firm: "No thanks. You're not needed. You're out of touch. Back to your room."

Your experience is your experience; it need be nothing more. Praise God for it. Embrace it. Revel in it.

This, then, is what we now know of contemplative vision, of your one and only, original, meditative, engaged way of viewing the world:

• It includes stillness and silence.
• It involves coming into the present, the now.
• It welcomes whatever comes through emptiness and receptivity.
• It notices, pays attention, and observes.
• It recognizes that what and how you see is uniquely yours and worth embracing, expressing, and celebrating.

---

4. Dannielle Krysa and Martha Rich, *Your Inner Critic Is a Big Jerk: And Other Truths about Being Creative* (San Francisco: Chronicle Books, 2016).

For Reflection:

1. When have you experienced the dulling of direct experience through analysis and categorization? Try, today, at least once, to let "the experience be the experience."

2. How aware are you of the role your feelings play in your photography? Review some of your favorite images; what feelings do you associate with each? Peace? Joy? Desire? Puzzlement? Love? Tenderness? Hope? List and think about these.

3. Describe your unique contemplative vision.

CHAPTER 7

NO SUCH THING AS COMMONPLACE (NOTHING IS EXEMPT)

We are not interested in the unusual, but in the usual seen unusually.[1]

—*Beaumont Newhall*

Right in Front of You

With your photography, you have the capacity to make the ordinary extraordinary. Wherever you are with your camera, if you say, "There's nothing here to photograph," then you're not paying attention. You may think, for example, that your home is the epitome of the commonplace—your furnishings, your knick-knacks, the pillows on the couch, the dishes in the cupboard, the stuff stored on your bathroom counter, the toys scattered on your kid's bedroom floor, the tools in your garage—what's interesting about these? Contemplative vision tells us, "A lot."

I have said to friends, "Give me an hour or two to roam your home with my camera, and I guarantee to surprise you with the beauty, mystery, thoughtfulness, and art to be found there." "Yeah, right," they say, skeptical. But, indeed, I have done this in over a dozen homes over the years, and the results have been surprising, revealing, beautiful, at times moving.

On the next page is one example from a friend's home in San Francisco. The photo is of a glass globe on a table in his parlor. I'm not sure how the sphere is constructed, nor the optical science at work, but the result, for me, is most satisfying.

---

1. Beaumont Newhall, *Focus: Memoirs of a Life in Photography* (Boston: Bullfinch, 1993), 122.

The small inner sphere, crystal clear, hangs suspended in the greater, watery globe. The inner sphere functions as a lens, itself

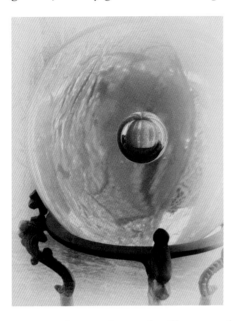

capturing an image of the embroidered drapes hanging in the front window beyond the table. I feel a sense of mystery in this photograph . . . and nostalgia, even though it's not my globe nor my home. I love the contrast of clarity and soft blur. I sense both stillness and tension . . . what holds the inner sphere frozen in place? Will it remain there, quiet in the center? Is there a metaphor here, something about my own inner place of stillness and clarity, where it lives, and what keeps it in place? It's just a photo of a glass ball on a table in someone's house, or *is* it?

As a contemplative photographer, you have the skills to stop and see what others may miss. You know that to be still and silent, to come into the present moment, to receive, to attend and observe, to honor your own perceptions, all of this primes you for contemplative vision. You are ready, now, to see the extraordinary all around you, or, as Beaumont Newhall said in our opening quote for this chapter: you are ready to see the usual *unusually*.

How about trying that right now? Wherever you are at this moment, stop to breathe deeply, center, focus, relax, and open. Look around you. Allow the objects in your field of vision to reach out to you; some are inviting you to attend to them. Which engage you? What connects with you? Is it color, either vibrant or muted? Is it pattern or texture—rough, smooth, rounded, edgy? Are feelings triggered by certain objects, feelings like amusement, warmth, curiosity, or distaste? Are you noting the play of light on, in, or through objects? Where are there interesting shadows? Do you see pleasing shapes? Disturbing shapes? Unusual shapes? Do you observe instances of juxtaposition, like a tablet or smart phone resting on an antique table, or pets sleeping peacefully with the TV droning behind them? Start framing photographs with your mind's eye; how could you capture what you see, feel, observe through the lens of a camera? See unusually. See the extraordinary, right here, right within reach.

Here are two examples of the ordinary made extraordinary in photographs from my own home.

The first photo is of an oscillating fan. Note the play of light and shadow, the interplay of pattern. The second is the music that happened to be open on the piano that day. Both are common, unremarkable items around the house, until seen with contemplative vision.

Wonder

Alchemy, it is said, changes common metal to gold. We do this (we contemplative photographers) with our cameras, transforming the ordinary and overlooked into images of *wonder*. Call it *photographic alchemy*.

To view the world with wonder is to see with the eyes of God.

I value *wonder*. Living in wonder means living in awe. Contemplative vision looks with wonder at the world and reels with amazement, gratitude, and love. Contemplative photography uses the camera to reveal the wonder everywhere around us, the wonder of the stars wheeling in the night sky, the wonder of a freshly opened box of crayons, the wonder of a human face, the wonder of billowing clouds and pounding surf, the wonder of touch, the wonder of sorrow, the wonder of abandoned houses, the wonder of family heirlooms, the wonder of creation, the wonder of life.

Wonder becomes an encounter with the holy, with the sacred, with that which provides meaning, what many call "God." To stand in awe, to be astonished by beauty, intricacy, splendor, kindness, trust, the now, is a deeply spiritual experience. "*Wow!*" becomes a confession of faith.

Remember when, as a child, wonder was your natural state? Each day was wonder-filled. A towering cloud, a fierce wind, geese crying overhead, the fire truck screaming by, the dioramas at a museum, the feel of mud oozing between your toes—a moment of wonder was one that stopped you, one in

which time stood still, and you were neither in the past nor the future; all was now.

Wonder is all the things we've talked about thus far related to contemplative vision. Wonder is a moment that lifts you up and out of this place, the familiar, the routine. Wonder takes the lid off, so you expand—soul, spirit, understanding. You enlarge. Something escapes that you can't recapture—nor would want to; it's a part of you that's longing to fly free.

To live with wonder is to live at the liminal edge, the place between this world and the next, the intersection of the known and the unknown, the natural and the supernatural, certainty and mystery, here and everywhere, now and eternity.

Welcome to wonder. Welcome to contemplative vision.

The Invitation

"Pay attention to me,"
says the flower.

"I am beautiful.
I am complex.
I am an invitation from Reality,
a message from somewhere sacred and serene.

"I am nature.
I am purity.
I am generosity and wholeness.
I am comfort and hope.
I am possibility.

"I am your wake-up call
and your warning,
the voice from deep within,
the voice calling through time."

"A flower," you acknowledge,
and slip it into its category,
one of a million dusty slots in your brain.
"Done," you say.

But the flower will not be silenced:
"Look at me.
Learn of yourself and God.
Look until your tension eases,
your heart opens,
your tears flow,
your healing begins."

"Pay attention to me,"
says the flower.

For Reflection:

1. Walk through your home, looking for ordinary objects that, with contemplative vision, could become extraordinary. List these here:

2. Pick up an object in your living room, dining room, kitchen, or bedroom. Spend at least three minutes just looking at it, turning it over, viewing it from various angles and in different light. What are you surprised to discover? In what ways are you seeing this "usual" object "unusually," as if for the first time?

3. What does it mean to you to "see with the eyes of God"? When does this happen for you? What can you do to nurture this part of your contemplative vision?

PART 2

THE PRACTICE OF CONTEMPLATIVE PHOTOGRAPHY

CHAPTER 8

THE BASIC TOOLS

When you begin viewing the world through your camera lens, your senses sharpen as your mind and eyes are forced to focus on people and things never before noticed or thought about. I discovered that even if I didn't always take a picture, the simple act of carrying a camera and searching for something to photograph greatly sharpened my powers of observation and allowed me to experience much more of life.[1]

—*Kent Reno*

Getting Started

All you really need is a *camera*. You can use a stand-alone camera, either film or digital, or you can use the camera incorporated into your smartphone or tablet. The quality of phone- and tablet-based cameras continues to improve, offering ever higher resolution and the addition of basic controls, like zoom, exposure, and focus.

A good stand-alone camera provides a greater range of control, from shutter speed to aperture, white balance to noise control, contrast to brightness. Do you need all that control? Not necessarily. It depends on your level of interest in fiddling, manipulating, and adjusting settings. If you find yourself stymied at times because your camera can't do things you wish it would do (and know a more sophisticated camera *could* do), then you might consider upgrading. But if you're satisfied with the images you're creating, stick with the camera you currently use. You may find satisfaction working within the limits of a specific camera, seeing what you can create within those boundaries, and, likewise, it can feel overwhelming to have a camera with

---

1. Kent Reno, "The Casual Observer: A Street Photographer's World View," *Camera & Darkroom* (August, 1994), 7.

so many controls and options that your head spins (and current cameras have hundreds of possible settings . . . and thousands of possible *combinations* of settings).

With a digital camera, we can take as many photos as we wish without worrying about cost. Back when film cameras were the only option, I carefully considered what I would photograph and how many pictures I would take, always knowing I would be paying to develop and print those photos. Where I once would have taken one or two shots of, say, an unfolding rose, now I take a dozen or two, varying the angle, exposure, focal point, lighting. Digital photography allows us to endlessly experiment . . . and by experimenting, to constantly improve. And with digital photography we can immediately review any photo we've taken. Does the result match our original perception? If not, adjust and take another . . . and another . . . and another.

You can pursue your interest in contemplative photography with nothing more than your camera, but most likely, you'll want to share those photos with others. You can share photos taken with your smartphone directly from the phone, either through e-mail or by posting to social media. Some stand-alone digital cameras now have that capability as well. For the rest of us, we will transfer our photos via cable, Wi-Fi, or memory cards to our computers, where we may do some digital clean-up and manipulation before sharing or printing them. So, obviously, the second most important piece of equipment would be your *computer*. The more involved the processing you'd like to do of your photos, the more powerful a computer you'll need.

Both the Mac and Windows operating systems include basic photo-editing software, and while much more sophisticated programs for working with photos are available, these basic programs provide quite a few options and may be all you need (or want).

We will look more at working with photos on your computer in a bit.

Today's inkjet *printers* offer an immediate and inexpensive way to print your own photos in sizes up to about 8" x 10".

Just about any inkjet sold today will accomplish this; almost all print in color and offer photo-printer settings. If you're currently looking for a printer and know you'll be printing photos, check the printer's specifications; while most printers will print photos, not all will be the quality you'd get from a printer specifically designed to provide quality photo printing.

So, to sum up, the basics you'll need in your contemplative photography toolbox include:

- a camera
- a computer
- and possibly a printer, if you'd like to print photos at home

Other Equipment

I own and regularly use several other tools as well. These are optional, and you may have others you consider essential that I don't. Here are my favorites:

A macro lens: A macro lens is a close-up lens, making it possible to get very close to your subject. My DSLR (digital single-lens reflex) camera allows me to swap out lenses; my basic lens is a standard zoom lens that came bundled with my camera, but I also have (and frequently use) a macro lens, making it possible to get photos such as this one, of a strawberry.

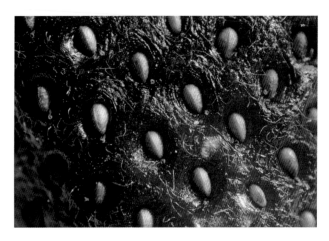

As in this case, close-up or macro photography reveals surprising detail about everyday objects. Most digital cameras, even those without interchangeable lenses, will include macro or close-up settings. If your camera has one, experiment with it, getting in close to see what new discoveries you make. If using a smartphone, look for a macro lens that clips over your phone's camera lens.

A tripod: A tripod makes it possible to get clear photos in circumstances where hand-holding the camera won't work. In dimmer light, for example, your camera may need a longer exposure, and holding it in your hands will result in a blurry photo (because of camera shake). Close-up and macro photography also often require the stability of a tripod, because at close quarters, even with a fast shutter speed, slight movement of the camera will change the precise focal point you've chosen. Tripods come in all sizes, from compact ones that fit in your pocket (and can stand on a table, wall, or nearby rock) to full-size ones that stand on the ground.

An external flash: Your camera or smartphone likely includes a built-in flash. This flash may fire automatically when the camera or phone decides that more light is needed for a well-lit photo, or it may be a flash you control, deciding for yourself when to supplement the natural light. Because the light from a camera or phone is very close to the camera's lens, the light hits your subject straight on, often "flattening" the resulting image, removing the shadows that occur with natural light and thus removing depth and texture. More pleasing and natural-looking images result with light coming from any direction but straight ahead.

An external flash can be either (a) attached to the camera, but aimed in different directions, so the light bounces off the ceiling or off a nearby wall, or (b) separated from the camera and placed wherever you wish, like off to one side of your subject or even behind it. Depending on your camera, the external flash may be controlled wirelessly, or it might be tethered to your camera with a cord. I have several external flashes that

I use for different situations, including a special "ring" flash that is exactly what it sounds like—a ring of light that mounts around the camera lens and is used primarily for macro shots, lighting the subject from all directions.

I find that most subjects I photograph look better with natural, existing light, not with a flash. Though there are definitely times when a flash is needed, and there are times when the creative use of flash yields unexpected and intriguing results, I don't use it very often. When I do, I'm very glad it gives me additional lighting options. I encourage you to experiment with whatever flash equipment you might have (or get).

A *studio tent/diffusion light box*: This goes by various names; it may also be called a light tent kit or a studio box. It's a lightweight, portable cube made of translucent, white cloth with one open side. You place your subject inside the cube, arrange external lights as you wish, typically one on each side, shining onto the white fabric sides of the cube. The fabric diffuses the light passing through onto your subject, providing a soft, even light. You take your pictures through the open side of the cube. These lighting kits usually come with two or more colored backdrops (like gray, blue, white, black) and work well for close-up and macro photos. Small ones are available for less than twenty dollars; larger, more versatile ones, that include lights on small stands to position as you wish, plus additional backdrops, can range up to one hundred dollars.

An *accessible guide to using my camera*: My go-to camera is a Nikon DSLR, which I've now owned for about three years. It's not a professional level camera, but what is sometimes referred to as a "prosumer" camera, somewhere between a full-featured DSLR preferred by professionals and a feature-rich point-and-shoot designed for consumers: *pro* + *sumer*. Even after three years, I still have moments when I feel frustrated when the camera refuses to do what I think it should be doing. So far, in every case, it turns out the problem isn't the camera, but me, which is why I own several guides to using my camera, a couple in print and one on my tablet. The smaller of the print guides conveniently fits in my camera bag. Your camera came with a manual, but in my experience, official camera manuals are rarely user-friendly. The manuals do cover everything, but not in a way that facilitates easy referencing. If your camera is complicated enough so that third-party publishers issue after-market guides, consider getting one. Trust me, it will help you maintain your contemplative state and stay in the flow.

The better you know your camera (and other equipment) the less likely you are to get sidetracked by the frustration of not having it function as you want it to function (and, as just mentioned, the easier it will be to stay contemplatively in the flow). If, in the field, I find myself having problems not getting the camera to behave as I'd like, I find it helpful to tell myself: "Okay, breathe. You don't need to do this now. Later, at home, look it up and see what's happening. For now, move on to something else. What other subject engages you?" For me, this works.

Extra batteries: This may seem like a no-brainer, but I can't tell you how many times I've had everything I need with me for the day's photo outing . . . except for that extra battery (or batteries). A half hour into it, with hours more to go (in theory), the adventure grinds to a halt because the spare lies at home on the kitchen counter where I'd just charged it. *Aargh*.

That's my photo toolbox. I keep other items handy, like lens cleaner, lens cleaning cloths, a lens brush (the kind with the rubber bulb that blows away dust), and extra memory cards. I like to use two filters, which screw onto the front of my camera lens—a UV filter (to block ultraviolet light) and a polarizing filter (to cut down on reflected light and glare).

Taking Photos, Creating Images

Now let's return to the issue of the digital manipulation of your photos, either in your phone or camera—before downloading the photos or sending them via e-mail or social media—or later once the photos have been moved to your computer. I know photographers who don't believe manipulation of images should be a part of the photographic process. They will say that you either take a good photo or you don't, and playing with the photos to "fix" or "alter" them isn't a legitimate part of the process.

The truth is, your camera or phone manipulates your photos before you see them displayed on your camera's monitor or your phone's screen, using algorithms to tweak your images to give you what the onboard computer thinks will yield the best photos. Even with film cameras, both the camera itself and the person processing the film and printing the photos in a darkroom or lab make multiple decisions that impact the final print. Ultimately, then, there's no such thing as an unmanipulated photograph; it's really a question of degree or extent.

I believe in letting your process be your process. If your goal is to get meaningful, contemplative photos purely with the taking of the pictures, with little or no processing afterwards, then I believe that's what you should do. If you find the creative process of working with images on the computer to also be satisfying—an extension of what you've done in the field— then include that in your process.

I speak of *taking photos*, then *creating images*. That's *my* process. I find the computer work to be every bit as challenging and creative as the field work. A great image always begins with a great photo, but that final image may look vastly different from the original photo. The entire process is mine. The entire process is creative. The entire process is satisfying. The same vision guides both the taking of photos and the creating of images. Sometimes, the final image is very close to the original photo, such that most people would be hard-pressed to see the difference. Other times the final image varies greatly. In either case, the final image reflects the world I see and imagine. Here, side by side, is an example of an original photo (on the left) and the final image (on the right).

So how do I get from the photo on the left to the photo on the right? I play (and "play" is the right word) in several photo manipulation programs. There are many. Windows 10 comes with a very basic program called Windows Photos. The Mac version, similarly called Photos, is more robust. Perhaps the ultimate in photo manipulation software is Adobe's Photoshop. I use a slimmed down version of Photoshop, also from Adobe, called Photoshop Elements, which includes most of what people use Photoshop to do, but with a much lower price tag. Other commercially available programs include Photo Reactor, PaintShop, PhotoPad, Luminar, FotoWorks XL, and PhotoDirector. In addition, many companies offer "plug-ins" for programs like Photoshop, Photoshop Elements, and Lightroom (another Adobe product for working with photos); a plug-in is a supplemental program that, once loaded on your computer, is accessible from within the host program (like Photoshop Elements). Many of these plug-ins also function as stand-alone programs. I use two extensively, those from On1

Software and those from Topaz Labs. The On1 stand-alone program is On1 Photo RAW. The full program from Topaz Labs is Topaz Studio.

There are also stand-alone programs that are not full editing programs, nor plug-ins, but programs providing a specific function. Dynamic Auto Painter applies filters to your photos that mimic classic art styles, including those of known artists like Van Gogh and O'Keefe. PhotoBlend helps you merge elements from various photos to create photo montages. Dynamic Photo HDR leads you through the creation of HDR photos—"high dynamic range" images that result from combining multiple images that are identical except taken at different exposure levels.

If you'd like a chance to experiment with a full photo-manipulation program without investing any money, there is a completely free and surprisingly robust program available for download called GIMP (an acronym for GNU Image Manipulation Program). A variety of third-party plug-ins boost GIMP's already impressive feature set.

For your phone or tablet, you'll also find a wide range of options for editing photos, though most of these programs will be more limited in what they can do (because of memory and processing limitations). For the iPhone, look into Snapseed, Touch Retouch, Afterlight, Enlight, Mextures, Camera+, and ProCamera. For Android phones, check out AirBrush, Photoshop Express, Pixlr, Aviary, Snapseed, Photo Lab, Cymera, Open Camera, PicsArt Photo Studio, and PhotoDirector.

This is just a sampling of available programs and apps to try if you're interested in playing more with your contemplative photos. In Part 4: Resources (p. 133) I list online links for all of these.

We conclude this chapter with two additional examples of images created using several of the above-mentioned programs:

A watercolor-like treatment of a box of pastel chalk.

A soft, impressionist view of autumn on Cherry Creek, in Denver.

For Reflection:

1. What tools do you have in your contemplative photography toolbox? What other tools (either mentioned above or others that you know of) would you like to try?

2. What are your thoughts or feelings on the "manipulation" of your photos? What have you done, to this point, in photo-manipulation programs? What might you like to try moving forward?

CHAPTER 9

A BASIC APPROACH

This Bud's for You

layers of wrapped tissue
translucent, fragile
shades of pale green
    and slight lavender
small bud,
barely larger than a match head,
growing solo among the ferns
beneath the trees, beside the lake

small grace,
unfolding wonder

Pulling It Together

This is the point when I pull together what we've explored about contemplative vision and share the simple process I follow when my hope/intent is to take photographs from a place of quiet, present receptivity. There aren't really steps to this process, except the obvious ones of choosing a location/subject and preparing your equipment. In fact, it's less a process and more the mental, emotional, and spiritual preparation similar to what one would do to prepare for worship or settle down for quiet prayer. It's more about *being* than *doing*, which makes sense if what we're attempting is a form of meditation.

So, yes, begin with deciding that you're ready to engage in the spiritual practice of contemplative photography. You want to do this for yourself, to connect with yourself in a deeper, calmer way, to have this time with God, to approach and more fully embrace some small part of God's amazing world. How much time will you set aside? How will you free yourself to focus on photography without distraction? How will you set aside—guard—this special time, which, really, is sacred time?

You then settle on where you'd like to be for this. Perhaps you have the house to yourself for a blessed—and unusual—hour or two; as we've seen, your home offers plenty of photo-worthy subjects to explore. Perhaps, while driving or walking earlier in the day, you noticed a certain stand of trees in the neighborhood, a barn in picturesque disrepair, or a restored hot rod in a neighbor's driveway. Perhaps you, like me, have several spots near home to which you gravitate for walks and quiet moments, like a public garden, a lakeshore, an art museum, a quaint neighborhood, a cluster of downtown skyscrapers, an old church, or a trail meandering along a stream. What draws you?

Once you arrive, do whatever it is you need to do to find your place of inner stillness, that place of present awareness (the here, the now), that openness to what comes to the forefront as you patiently wait. What yearns for your attention?

Then begin to notice. Let's imagine it's the holidays, the Christmas tree is freshly decorated, and I'm drawn to a particular ornament I see hanging toward the top, an ornament that once hung on my sister's tree, but became mine after she passed away. I think, "It *is* beautiful; I see why she bought it—it's graceful, unique, ethereal. Yes, I'm going to take some photos of that." But I don't immediately aim the camera and start clicking. I approach the ornament, taking a closer look at it than I have before. I take it off the tree and hold it in my hands, turning it over, viewing it from all angles, feeling its smoothness and lightness. It's round, clear glass, except where, while still hot, points on the exterior were pushed to the interior. Those points either already had molten blue glass added to the hot surface, or whatever tool was used to push in at those points was first dipped in molten blue glass. I place the ornament on the dining room table, with natural light behind it from the dining room window. I've connected with my subject—looked at it and felt it. I'm taking things slowly, allowing the time and space I need to notice, appreciate, and wonder. Now, intuitively, I feel ready to take some pictures.

And I do. I take quite a few, in fact. Below is my favorite from that afternoon of photography.

Is it just a Christmas ornament? I've been surprised what others— who did not get the explanation I offered above—see in it. None guess that it's a Christmas ornament. One sees it as a metaphor for the complexity of the human body—all nerves and muscles. Another sees water. I titled this image *Convergence*; it speaks to me of people and things coming together, as people and things are meant to do.

I continue taking photos, repeatedly pausing to connect, trying not to rush as I move on to another subject—another ornament, another flower, another view of the mountain, etc. I continue until I either run out of time, my energy flags, or I simply find nothing else calling for my attention.

Back at the Computer

A more established process awaits once I am at the computer and have downloaded my new images. Your process will differ from mine, depending on what you'd like to accomplish and what software you choose to use. For me, it looks something like this:

- I download the photos into Photoshop Elements Organizer. I look through the new photos, deleting the blurry ones, the boring ones, the mistakes, the ones I probably won't do anything with. I note the ones I find particularly pleasing. I ask myself, "Of the dozen or so photos you have of this particular subject, which two or three are worth keeping?" I delete some more. (This is an issue for me. Way too many photos live on my computer. The regular deletion of ones

I'll never use could be another spiritual practice . . . clearing out, letting go, decluttering.)

- I select a few pictures that I particularly like and open those in Photoshop Elements Editor, my first choice for editing. (Organizer and Editor are the two parts of the Photoshop Elements software package.)

- I do basic cleanup of these images, adjusting brightness and contrast, possibly tweaking color and sharpening, often cropping for a more pleasing composition. Photo-manipulation programs will do much of this for you at the click of a button, if you wish, but you can choose to do it manually, making your own adjustments.

- At this point, I may be happy with an image and simply save it. Or I may want to add some simple effects, like a vignette or a frame.

- Or I'll flat-out play with the image, experimenting with a host of other filter options and treatments available through the various software programs I own. I offer this taste of what one photo can look like when given four different treatments; meet our cat Romeo:

If such playing with photos intrigues you, give it a try.

What you do with your final images is up to you. Maybe you keep them to yourself. Maybe you share them on Facebook or some other social media site. Maybe you'll print a few to frame and display in your home or office. In any case, may every one of them celebrate and honor your unique, contemplative vision.

Reflect and Consider

From time to time, you may want to sit with a photo you find particularly pleasing (or calming, challenging, healing) and consider why that image holds meaning for you. I offer these questions to guide your reflection:

- What drew me to this subject?
- What pleases me about this image?
- What am I feeling as I connect with this image?
- What surprises me about this image?
- What do I learn about *myself* from this image? What do I learn about the *world?* about *God?* about *desire? beauty? pain? healing? hope?*
- In what way does this image serve as a metaphor?
- Based on my response, what might I title this image?

Whether or not you engage in such reflection is totally up to you. As I've said before, the process needs only be the process, without explanation or analysis.

For Reflection:

1. The next time (or the first time) you intentionally take contemplative photos, how will you free yourself to focus without distraction? What can you do to set aside—and guard—this sacred time?

2. If you haven't yet begun your contemplative photography, identify settings where you'd like to start. If you've already started, what are your favorite places to take photos? What draws you to these places?

3. If you haven't yet explored photo manipulation programs, how interested are you in doing so? What would you hope would result?

PART 3

A DOZEN INVITATIONS

CHAPTER 10

PHOTOGRAPHY WITHOUT THE CAMERA

Seeing, in the finest and broadest sense, means using your senses, your intellect, and your emotions. It means encountering your subject matter with your whole being. It means looking beyond the labels of things and discovering the remarkable world around you.[1]

—*Freeman Patterson*

In this chapter and the chapters that follow, I extend to you a dozen invitations to contemplative, engaged photography. These invitations share one thing: all invite you to exercise your contemplative vision. Each will lead you into silence and mindfulness, open you to receive insight, hone your observational skills, and/or help you see the extraordinary in the ordinary.

I thought of calling these *assignments*, but that sounded too academic. I considered calling them *challenges*, but that sounded too assertive. I simply invite. I hope you enjoy them— and that they inspire you. They appear here in no particular order, nor do they build on each other, so dig in wherever you wish. And you will actually get more than a dozen, since I offer a few variations for most of them.

Before you start, do you recall the simple prayer I shared in chapter 3 that I repeat in walking meditation?

Spirit of God,
in this moment,
present with you,
help me to *be*.

---

1. Freeman Patterson, *Photography and the Art of Seeing* (Toronto: Key Porter Books, 2004), 7.

You might modify it as you approach each invitation, changing the final word, *be*, to *see*:

Spirit of God,
in this moment,
present with you,
help me to *see*.

This is my contemplative photographer's prayer . . . and my prayer for you.

You Are a Camera, Too

The lens in your eye functions as does the lens in your camera, taking in light and focusing that light as an image on the back of your eye, just as the light from the camera's lens focuses the light on the camera's sensor. Your optic nerve then sends that info to your brain for processing, just as the circuitry in your camera sends the info to your camera's onboard computer. Your brain processes the image and "displays" it in your mind's eye for your viewing, just as the camera's computer displays the image on the digital screen on the back of the camera. As sophisticated as the technology may be in the camera, it is nothing compared to the technology of your eye, your nervous system, and your brain. You are the ultimate camera.

You can sharpen your contemplative photography skills by using yourself—your eyes, your brain—as the camera. Walk around your home, your neighborhood, or your place of employment and "take pictures" using only your "camera self." Frame images. When you see something you like, think (or even say aloud), "Click" or "Beep." Mentally take the picture, then continue.

Observe what's happening. You are, among other things, developing your photographer's eye. I find that the more I take pictures, the more I look at everything in terms of the potential for photos. No matter where I am, that increasingly becomes my default way of viewing my surroundings. This exercise encourages that way of looking as you move through your day.

You are also, like someone on a film crew, "scouting" for possible locations, so, after spending some time framing images with your "camera self," you may want to return to take some of those pictures with your camera or phone.

Perhaps most importantly, you observe, you notice, you pay attention, you engage, you connect. You see contemplatively.

Through the Frame

When leading workshops on contemplative photography, I hand each participant a standard picture mat, the kind you can buy at a craft store to use when framing your own photos. Most of these have a 5" x 7" opening, with an exterior dimension of 8" x 10". I then ask everyone to stand up and move about the room, using the mat to frame possible photos. We experiment with holding the mats close to our faces, which results in a broad area being framed through the mat, with lots of visual content. We then hold the mats at arm's length, frame additional photos, and note how much narrower the scope is. Next, we move about the room, placing the mats flat against objects, framing potential close-ups, looking for interesting textures, colors, patterns.

If you don't have a precut mat at home with which to try this, simply cut an opening in a piece of stiff cardboard. Walk around the house experimenting with framing. Try reframing the same object from different angles, from close in to farther away. Try holding your mat flat against wallpaper or upholstery fabric; what interesting compositions can you create? What results when you frame only a part of an object, frame something off-center, or frame in such a way that someone else looking at such a photo wouldn't know what it was?

Again, as when "taking pictures" using only your "camera self," you are developing your photographer's eye, discovering possible subjects right in your home, and strengthening your observational skills. And, for a time at least, were you not centered in the moment . . . and enjoying it?

For Reflection:

1. After experimenting with either of these activities—"taking pictures" without your camera and using a precut mat to frame possible pictures—what have you learned about the photographer's eye? About *your* photographer's eye?

2. These activities also draw our attention to what we typically overlook. What have you discovered about the photographic potential of the "ordinary" in your home, neighborhood, or place of business?

3. Based on either (or both) of these activities, list subjects you've found that you now would like to photograph.

CHAPTER 11

SINGLE-ELEMENT STUDY

One of the magical things about photography is the transformation that takes place when you photograph something. Something that inherently has very little going for it, in terms of interest you take in it, can become infinitely more interesting when rendered as a photograph.[1]

—*Grant Mudford*

The Elements

A variety of elements make up a photograph, among them:

- color
- texture
- pattern
- shape/form
- light and shadow
- juxtaposition

Most pictures combine two or more of these elements, but fascinating and surprising images can feature or stress just one.

In this activity, I invite you to choose one of more of the elements listed above to explore with your camera . . . and, of course, with your singular, contemplative vision. You don't need to go far afield for this; opportunities abound for most of these in or around your home. Let's examine each of these individually, as well as view examples.

---

1. M. J. Rodriguez, "Grant Mudford: Finding His Niche in the Fine Arts World," *Photographer's Forum* (May 1993), 43.

Color

We live in a world of color. Color abounds in nature—in flowers, birds, blue skies, sunrises and sunsets, the greens and blues of lakes, oceans, and rivers, in the greens of grasses and forests, the browns, greys, and reds of earth and rocks. We fill our homes with color—walls, carpeting, furniture, accessories. We clothe ourselves in color—visit your closet to observe the variety of colors. Color soothes us, excites us, calms us, entertains us. We code color as well—red suggests danger; green reflects growth; blue eases, refreshes; shades of brown ground us. We each experience our own unique reaction to colors, to combinations of colors, to the presence or absence of certain colors. Its difficult to imagine living in a black-and-white world.

I suggest several ways to explore color as a function of contemplative photography.

One, choose a color and see how many images you can capture that feature that color. Do you have a favorite color? You could start with that, but any color will do. Find and photograph as many different items of that color as you can. I encourage you to move close in for this, so that the color fills the frame. Here, for example, are two images I found when looking for items that were red (and you can add to these the strawberry on page 48).

Two, look for items that reflect a wide range of colors, all in one place. I love to take this kind of photo and have found inspiration in a newly opened box of Crayola Crayons (the sixty-four-count box, with built-in sharpener), in my great-niece's bin of sidewalk chalk, in a pack of colored construction paper, in a table loaded with tubes of acrylic paints, and in a tray of kids' watercolor paints, shown here.

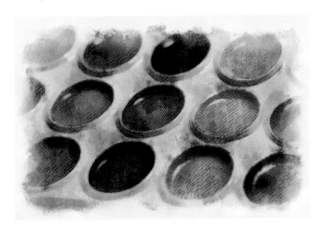

Third, look for subjects that combine colors. They may be colors that complement each other, colors that compete (perhaps jarringly), colors that please, colors that play well together and those that don't. Here's a colorful table and chairs at an outdoor café.

What do your photos of *color* say about your world? Your interests? Your growing awareness? The beauty of the ordinary?

Texture

Texture is all about touch. If I see a photo and have the desire to touch whatever is pictured, that's texture. If I see a photo and have the opposite reaction—the thought of touching the pictured object makes me cringe—that's texture too. Rough, smooth, coarse, bumpy, dimpled, sharp, spiny, fuzzy, hairy—texture surrounds us. All fabrics have texture, as do plants and human skin. Furniture, floors, walls, railings, food, pets, all things have their unique "feel."

Look around you for interesting textures. "Feel" them with your eyes, then through your camera lens. See how many varied textures you can photograph in a given amount of time. Again, to capture texture, come in close; help us feel it. Here is an example:

What do your photos of *texture* say about your world? Your interests? Your growing awareness? The beauty of the ordinary?

Pattern

To find patterns, look for visual repetition. Patterns, too, show up everywhere: the plaids, checks, and stripes in your clothes, for example, or the individual steps in a flight of stairs. From where I sit as I type, I see patterns in the repeated boards in our wood floor, in the slats of the window blinds, in the molded vents on the side of the modem, in the embossing on the band of my Fitbit, in the stained-glass shade of the light fixture overhead, in the grain of the wood of the corner cabinet, in the slots of the return air vent on the wall, in the black-and-white keys of the piano—*everywhere.*

From where you sit right now, how many patterns can you identify? Which could you photograph?

This example features the windows of a Chicago high-rise.

What do your photos of *patterns* say about your world? Your interests? Your growing awareness? The beauty of the ordinary?

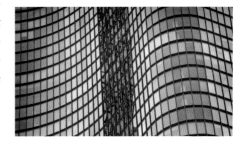

Shape/Form

Pleasing, intriguing shapes surround us as well. They may be rounded or angular, curvy or sleek, skewed or squared. What shapes draw and engage you? In nature, I love the bud of a rose, the stark, bare branches of a tree in winter, the curling fronds of a fern. At home, I delight in the curves of a hand-blown glass bowl, the spiraling metal ribbons of a light fixture, the plump roundness of a white ceramic water pitcher. Shapes and forms often have a satisfying soulfulness to them. From where you sit, what shapes and forms speak to you? Which would you like to photograph?

The key to capturing decent photos of shape and form is often to simplify the composition of the picture so the shape is isolated and stands apart. Coming in close helps, as does eliminating background distractions. I managed to do this in this photo, which celebrates simple yet appealing forms; it highlights the edges of nested glass bowls in a museum gift shop:

What do your photos of *shapes* and *forms* say about your world? Your interests? Your growing awareness? The beauty of the ordinary?

Light and Shadow

One element sits solidly at the heart of every photograph: *light*.

If there were no light, there would be no photography. A photograph *is* the embrace of light. Look around you; the play of light on and through objects, the shadows cast by light, the contrast of light and dark, the way light affects your mood—opportunities for soulful photography abound.

In the example to the right, late-afternoon sunlight casts shadows on a downtown Denver sidewalk.

I am often drawn to the mystery created by light and shadows. This photo, taken in the mountains of North Carolina, captures the early morning light breaking over the lake; I love the misty, mystical feel of the image below.

Where will you go to capture the dance of *light* and *shadow*? What do your photos of light and shadow say about your world? Your interests? Your growing awareness? The beauty of the ordinary?

Juxtaposition

In juxtaposition, you combine contrasting elements that "comment" on each or two elements that strike you as odd together. Such images lend themselves to thoughtful discussion: What's the message in this picture? Why does this feel jarring? What's going on here?

I find I either must create the opportunity for such an image by staging it, often as an intentionally provocative still life (imagine for example, a ripe tomato with several large, rusty nails stuck into it), or I unexpectedly stumble upon instances of juxtaposition out in the field. I have two examples of the latter.

In the first, we see classic New York City architecture from the early twentieth-century reflected in a brand-new, glass-encased office tower. Only the streetlight grounds the composition. The juxtaposition of the two time periods reflects the fact that we can only view the past through the perspective of the present.

In the second photo, also from New York, we view a church's cross through a loop of razor wire. *Ouch.* What's the message here about the Church? About American culture? About our own hearts?

Such images can be challenging both to the one taking the picture and to the one who views the image later. Where have you found opportunities to photograph instances of juxtaposition? What do your photos of *juxtaposition* say about your world? Your interests? Your growing awareness?

For Reflection:

1. These invitations ask you to attend closely to the world around you and to appreciate and honor the richness in simple, often overlooked aspects of our environment—color, texture, pattern, etc. How has taking photographs in response to this invitation heightened your awareness of such details? Your appreciation for them? Your pleasure in them?

2. What have you learned about your own relationship to color? To texture and pattern? To form? To light and shadow? To juxtaposition? Where have you found God in these exercises?

CHAPTER 12

SINGLE-SUBJECT STUDY

The photographer projects himself into everything he sees, identifying himself with everything in order to know it and to feel it better.[1]

—*Minor White*

Up Close and Personal

When, in chapter 3, we explored the concept of "flow," I shared the story of my encounter with the dahlias at the Denver Botanic Gardens. In particular, I focused in on one bloom and took pictures of it from directly above, from the sides, from underneath. I observed how, as my viewing angle changed, the light and shadow on the flower changed, offering new and different effects. At times I worked close-up, with my macro lens, then switched to my standard lens and took additional photos from farther back. I experimented with different backgrounds, like the blue sky and other blooms. By the time I was done, I knew that single dahlia very well.

This is called a "single-subject study," and I invite you to try the same. It gives you the opportunity to really, truly see something in a way you haven't before. Whatever the object you choose—a flower, a vase, a carton of eggs, a child's toy, an old pair of sneakers, a bolt of fabric—spend time photographing it from varying angles and distances, experimenting with adjustments on your camera (to the extent your camera and skills allow), working with different lighting in different settings. You will deepen your appreciation for that object. You may consider more intentionally its history, the role it plays in someone's life (yours, for example), its color, texture, and

---

1. Susan Sontag, *On Photography* (New York: Doubleday, 1989), 116.

form. The ordinary becomes extraordinary when you honor it in this way.

I came away from my "quality time" with that dahlia thinking, "Dahlias are amazing . . . and *God's* amazing."

Even better, you will likely end up with some very interesting, surprising, satisfying photographs, as I did with that single dahlia.

Samples

I engage in single-subject photographic studies quite often. It not only provides an opportunity to deeply connect with a subject, but also, because of the variety of shots I'm taking, results in multiple satisfying images.

Here is one example of my single-subject studies. I offer three images of my Mickey Mouse watch, which has both a clear face and back so one can watch the movement of the inner mechanism.

A Few Suggestions

My samples shown on the previous page were taken with my larger camera, using my macro lens. My subject was relatively small, so coming in close made sense. Your subject may be a large one, and not require close-up work, but I do suggest, whatever your subject, you move in close for a few of the shots. I've done this activity with our cats and ended up with very tight (and striking) images of a single, intense eye, the translucent interior of an ear, and the pads of one foot. *Revealing.* While a good picture may include the entire subject, an even better picture may focus in on a portion, a detail, an intriguing part of the whole.

Give yourself permission to go a little crazy with the number of pictures you take. You will likely end up with only a few that please you, but that's the beauty of digital photography. Experiment all you like.

Don't limit yourself to subjects that you perceive as pretty or photo-worthy. Challenge yourself to tackle something ordinary that you might overlook.

If you know a friend or family member has a fondness for a specific object in their life, like a stuffed animal from childhood or a family heirloom, consider honoring that fondness by undertaking a single-subject photographic study of that object. If you can do so without their knowledge, all the better. Combine your best images into a collage or booklet, then give it as a gift.

For Reflection:

1. Look around your home or neighborhood. List possible subjects for a single-subject study. Look beyond the obvious.

2. Once you've conducted a single-subject photographic study, review the results. What have you learned about your subject? What pleases you about what you've captured?

CHAPTER 13
SINGLE-LOCATION STUDY

The place on which you are standing is holy ground.

—*Exodus 3:5* NRSV

All Ground Is Holy Ground

We take what I call a "photo walk." I lead a small group—all equipped with cameras or smartphones—on an excursion to various locations at Kanuga, an Episcopal conference center and camp in the mountains of North Carolina. We visit a shady outdoor chapel (named for St. Francis) built alongside a stream, then the main lodge with its massive stone fireplace, and end up stopping on a walkway between a cluster of cottages on one side and the historic Chapel of the Transfiguration, dedicated in 1942, on the other. I invite participants to spread out a bit so they're not standing shoulder to shoulder. Then I give them this invitation (which I will soon extend to you as well): "I would like you to stay right where you are. You may turn around, but you may not move to another location. From this location, take at least ten uniquely different photographs." They look at me like I'm crazy. I say, "You can do this. Look up; look down; look side-to side; stand, sit, squat, or kneel . . . *but remain in the same spot.* Take as many photos as you'd like but strive to get ten pictures of *different* subjects."

I stand back and watch. Initially participants look puzzled, but after looking around for a moment or two, their contemplative vision kicks in, and they begin to *see.* They raise their cameras and start taking pictures. They turn. *Click.* They kneel. *Click.* They get "aha" looks. *Click.* They may sit for a bit. *Click.* They suddenly notice each other. *Click, click.* They look at me and smile. I'm already smiling.

After about ten minutes, I invite everyone to gather and to reflect on what they just experienced. To a person, they all express surprise and gratitude. I ask them to review their new pictures and each to share one or two favorites. We see pictures of trees towering overhead, of ants busy around an anthill, of a joint in the split rail fence, of flowers blooming beside the chapel, of the shady entrance to a cottage, of another participant engrossed in her picture-taking, of a participant's wedding ring sparkling in the sun, of a hand cradling a pine cone, of a stained-glass window in the chapel, of the textured siding of the chapel, of one participant's sandaled feet . . .

I pick up on the photo of the sandaled feet. "That reminds me," I say, "of God's instruction to Moses to take off his sandals, because he was standing on holy ground. Through this activity, the ground where we stand now has become holy ground."

A participant says, "I believe all ground is holy ground . . . or can be."

We all agree.

Discovering Your Holy Ground

The problem with extending this invitation to you now, through this book (instead of in person), is that you have been alerted to the "surprise" element that I can pull off with unsuspecting participants. *If* you have your camera or phone beside you right now, I say, "*Surprise. From wherever you are—right at this moment*—take at least ten uniquely different photos. You may turn around if you wish, kneel, sit, lie down, but stay in the same spot."

If you do *not* have your camera within reach, then I trust you to find a spot from which you would typically *not* think of taking pictures and to spend ten minutes there transforming that location into "holy ground." How about the middle of your kitchen? The workshop in the garage or basement? Your patio, balcony, or porch? A corner of your yard? The lobby of your condo/apartment building? A park bench? An aisle of your grocery store? The bedroom of a family member? A street corner on your way to work?

A single-location photographic study provides an ideal place to discover the extraordinary in the ordinary, to see the usual unusually, to focus your singular contemplative vision on everyday places—on *remarkable* everyday places. All places, all moments offer the possibility of discovery, wonder, connection, and meaning. What will *you* find?

Holy Ground

Wherever you stand
is holy ground.

Take off your shoes,
that is,
discard whatever keeps you
from direct contact
with the something greater
that waits for you.

Take off your shoes
    because wherever you stand
is holy ground,
the ground of possibility,
the ground of much more.

For Reflection:

1. What does this activity reveal to you about what you consider a "photo-worthy" location?

2. Once you've conducted a single-location study, reflect on how this activity deepens your contemplative vision.

3. Review the results of your single-location photographic study. What do you learn about the incredibly varied world around you? About yourself? About God? What pleases you about the pictures you've taken?

CHAPTER 14

CLOSE-UPS AND MACROS

When your subject finally touches (or almost touches) the edges of the frame, the close-up encounter can finally begin, and from there, if you so choose, it can become even more intimate by your simply moving in even closer . . .[1]

—*Bryan Peterson*

Discovering What Was There All Along

I am a big fan of *close-up* and *macro* photography. Close-up and macro photography reveal unexpected worlds in the intricate details of "the small" . . . or in isolated portions of "the large." All of the elements of a photograph (explored in chapter 11)—color, form, texture, pattern, and so on—become intensely evident when you move in closer with your camera.

I tend to use the terms close-up and macro interchangeably, but technically, they refer to two different things. *Close-up* means taking a photo of something at close range. The images of flowers found on pages 15 and 40 provide examples of close-up photos. *Macro* is used to described extreme close-up photography. The image of the strawberry (p. 48) and the images of my Mickey Mouse watch (p. 78) are examples of macro photography. Generally speaking, macro photography is a subset of close-up photography.

Many cameras offer a close-up setting; if selected, the camera adjusts various parameters in the camera to make the best of photos taken at close range. A dedicated macro lens (sometimes also called a micro lens) provides the more extreme magnification needed to take macro photos. (There *are* other ways

---

1. Bryan Peterson, *Understanding Close-Up Photography: Creative Close Encounters with or without a Macro Lens* (New York: Amphoto Books, 2009), 124.

to get closer without a macro lens, like using extension tubes or close-up filters. If you're curious, research these online.)

If you look back at the photos included as examples in this

book, my love for close-up photography reveals itself. Such photos—and the pursuit of them—lead me to a place of wonder; I find beauty, delight, and playfulness in revealing what lies right under our noses but goes unseen. Or what *crawls* right under our noses, like this colorful beetle making its way across a hot sidewalk.

Close-Up and Macro Tips

In reviewing my close-up photos, looking for samples to share in this chapter, I came away amazed at how many options I had. I stopped looking once I had listed about fifty possibilities; there were several hundred more to choose from. From flowers and fruits/vegetables, to insects and pets, to holiday ornaments and toys/games, to kitchen tools and friends' fingers and toes—there isn't much I turn down when given the chance to examine and experiment with a close-up setting or a macro lens. I encourage you to be just as non-discriminating; nearly anything you get close to could result in a startling, pleasing, or fascinating image.

Close-up photography—and especially macro photography—requires a steady hand or a tripod. The closer you get to your subject the more camera shake will impact the quality of the photo. Additionally, the depth of field shrinks as you move in. Depth of field is how much of the image will be in focus. Note the picture here of the gingerbread men in their white chocolate pants; only one of them is in focus. This isn't a bad thing:

you get to decide where to place that focus, and in doing so, you lead the viewer's eye into your image. If photographing a flower, for example, the one clear portion of your photo might be a single petal or the pistil and stamen at the center of the bloom. Pay attention to your point of focus.

You get close to your subject in two ways. First, you can physically move the camera closer to the subject. Second, you can use the zoom function of your camera. Most cameras without interchangeable lenses feature some degree of zoom. Lenses for interchangeable lens cameras come in two flavors, fixed (meaning the lens has one focal length) or zoom (meaning the lens offers multiple focal lengths). Experiment with both ways of getting closer to your subject. Using your zoom to get close will result in a shallower depth of field, so less of your subject will be in focus. You may want that, or you may not, so try it different ways to see what results.

Because close-up photography restricts your depth of field, the background of your image will blur, as seen in the first photo on the next page of Christmas lights on a railing. Only the single, closest bulb is in focus, but you recognize the other spots of white behind it as additional lights on the same string. This is a desirable effect. Pay attention to—and take advantage of—what might appear in the background of your close-up and macro shots. The right background, hazy and blurred, adds visual interest . . . and perhaps a bit of mystery. When taking close-up pictures of a flower, for example, blossoms of contrasting colors in the background appear as blurs, adding depth, providing balance and visual interest, and helping your subject stand out more dramatically.

Don't hesitate to get so close to your subject that its identity is lost. No one looking at the image below has been able to tell me what it is. Can you? This is a tea ball (in which one puts loose tea for brewing), opened flat on a light table. (A light table is a white, glass panel illuminated from below.) What possessed me to take a photo of a tea ball? I don't know—it was just there; when I opened the kitchen drawer, it said, "Hey, how about me?" And I'll never again view the tea ball as just another mundane object stuck in the

corner of a drawer. It has form and texture. When seen with contemplative vision, it becomes a thing of beauty, not only of function.

My love for close-up and macro photography stems from my delight in finding wonder and beauty in the intimate encounter with the simplest of objects. God lives where we find wonder and beauty, and thus the potential exists to find God everywhere.

For Reflection:

1. What are your favorite subjects to photograph close up? Which of your close-up photos are your favorites?

2. Walk through your house, looking in drawers or cabinets. Pull out five or six items that could result in interesting close-up or macro photos. Spend some time photographing them. What strikes you about the resulting images?

3. What do you learn about God from your work with close-up photography?

CHAPTER 15

VISUAL METAPHORS

> Meaningful art—in any medium—is mind changing, challenging the prejudices of conventional thought. In this role, art lives between the known and the unknown, communicating what it discovers in this ambiguous territory.[1]
>
> —*Phillippe L. Gross and S. I. Shapiro*

All of Life Is Metaphor

If you know me long enough, eventually you will hear me assert: *All of life is metaphor.* If we remain open, we discover truths about God, creation, people, self, life, and faith, for example, around us in the sights, sounds, and occurrences of daily life. You watch a mother's tender reaction when her child's ice-cream cone drops to the hot pavement; in her action you see God's concern for you in your everyday disappointments. As you attempt to hang a picture, you drop the nail—*for the fourth time*—and start to laugh; *so* like life, this need to keep trying, keep trying, persist. Your dog waits until you momentarily step out of the kitchen to go up on her hind legs to snatch a raw burger off the counter; "Yup, that's me," you observe, when you think of how often you wait to indulge your current vice until you believe you're unobserved. There is something of the Rorschach test operating here, where we project personal meaning onto events, but such meaning often needs to surface and is appropriate to welcome. *All of life is metaphor.*

People with contemplative vision tend to view life metaphorically. They open themselves to the possible connections between objects, self, others, and God. Contemplative photographers, whether they realize it or not, take photos that explore

---

1. Philippe L. Gross and S. I. Shapiro, *The Tao of Photography: Seeing Beyond Seeing* (Berkeley, CA: Ten Speed Press, 2001), vii.

these connections, and in them, find meaning. Things and events serve as symbols, even allegories or parables.

In this chapter, I invite you to create photographic metaphors.

Start by reviewing at least a dozen of your favorite contemplative photos; you may discover that you have already created a number of powerful metaphors. Look at each photo individually as you ask:

- Beyond the literal image, what deeper meaning do I find in this photo?
- In what ways does this photo provide comfort? Challenge? Hope? Peace? Why?
- How might this photo be a metaphor for my life right now? For the state of the world? For my relationship with God? With myself? With friends and family members?

This won't be true for all photos. It will be true for some.

It could be true for more. See what new photos you can take that "say something." Be as subtle or overt as you wish.

Samples

To inspire you, I offer a few examples from my own practice of meditative photography.

Among my top ten favorite photographs is this one, of a tree on the edge of a cliff in Arkansas. Its title? *Solitude.* This image speaks to me of standing tall, standing above, standing contentedly alone, standing strong despite exposure to the worst assaults of nature. This contemplative, metaphoric photo represents me at

my best. I am a lover of silence and solitude, and this tree and I stand together.

I enjoy walking, writing, and taking photographs in cemeteries. Cemeteries offer refuge for introverts and solitudes. No one talks much, traffic is at a minimum, and there are plenty of interesting things to observe and photograph, from gravestones to wildlife, from landscaping to historical artifacts. The photo below, taken in late winter in a cemetery in Colorado Springs, Colorado, functions metaphorically to me. Before I describe my take on it, what do you see in this image? The markers are for soldiers killed in war—hundreds of them. This alone sobers me. But the unique shadow cast by the barren tree behind me looks like either the creeping spread of an infection beneath the skin or blood flowing and spreading out from a wound. This shadowy web connects the graves; it holds all in its grasp. These are not pleasant associations, I acknowledge, but they lend the image power, reflecting the horror and pervasive, spreading destructiveness of war. I honor those whose graves I have photographed, even as I recognize that they, with their sacrifice, could not escape the loss and sorrow of the war in which they served.

To be honest, when I took these photos, I wasn't thinking deep thoughts about their potential meaning; I simply took what my contemplative vision led me to hope would be good photos. It was when later viewing them that I realized, wow, there's something more going on here for me. Which is not to say that I don't intentionally take metaphorical photos or that you shouldn't try. The more you work and play from your unique contemplative vision, the more opportunities you will see and the more often metaphor will emerge even when not your primary intention.

I offer these examples to inspire you and to kick-start the creative, metaphorical way you might look at selected pictures you have taken or will take. Invite God to engage with you in this; after all, this metaphorical world of ours springs from God's great, playful imagination.

For Reflection:

1. What does the statement *All of life is metaphor* mean to you? To what extent have you experienced this?

2. As you review some of your contemplative photos, looking for deeper meaning, what metaphorical themes do you observe? What do these say about you? Your faith?

3. Share a few of your metaphorical photos with a few friends or family members. Before telling them what meaning *you* find in the photos, invite them to share their thoughts and feelings. Then share yours and discuss.

CHAPTER 16

TELLING A STORY

Yes,
this may look like a photograph of a purple iris,
   a fishing pier,
   a weathered door frame,
   a ripe strawberry,
   a rain-streaked window,
but really,
it's a picture of my soul.

Your Photos Tell Your Story

Every photograph tells a story. Every photograph tells the photographer's story. A single photo may provide just a word, a phrase, a sentence, or a paragraph of that story. A handful of related photos may tell the story of a trip, an outing, or an event. A lifetime of photos becomes an autobiography. Every one of your photos contributes something to the overall tale of who you are, what you value, where you wander, when you struggle, why you live. Your photos tell your story, and others (potentially) know you through your photos.

When I reached the point when I felt ready to exhibit my images in a public venue (it happened to be a popular Denver coffee shop), the reality of this truth—*my photos tell my story*—hit home. I approached the installation of the display with a mixture of excitement and terror: this is me, on display; not just my photos hang here on these walls, *I* hang on these walls: "Here, take a look at my naked self, hanging here, you random strangers having coffee and working on your laptops. Will you ignore me? Laugh at me? Admire me?" Note that I wasn't asking, "Will you ignore my photos? Laugh at my photos? Admire my photos?" It felt more personal than that.

The first invitation I extend in this chapter is to gather two or three dozen of your favorite photos and to view them as *your story*. Don't limit these to photos you see as meditative or contemplative; choose *any* photos, because *all* of your photos illustrate your story, including those quick shots of that recent birthday party. If this collection of photos was handed to someone who knew nothing about you, what story would it tell? What might that stranger say?

- Ah, what I learn about the photographer is . . .
- Here is a woman who likes . . .
- Here is a man who believes in . . .

I suggest you do this for yourself, trying, as you do, to look objectively at these images. Even better, with the help of a friend or family member, arrange for a stranger to reflect on a set of your photos; this would be, obviously, someone known to your friend or family member, but not to you. Either way, what story do your photos tell?

Photographic Storytelling

Understanding the storytelling power of photography—a power at work even when unintended—you can also use your photos to tell an original, self-contained story, a story that has spiritual meaning for you, a story you create or observe unfolding. Perhaps you will tell a story of love or compassion, or of hope or despair, or of sorrow or loss, or of companionship or solitude, or of exploration or discovery. Will you tell your story with inanimate objects? With pets and/or people? Will a series of four pictures adequately tell the story? A dozen pictures? Two dozen pictures? Free your imagination; be creative. There's no possibility of failure here. You are engaging (with God's creative Spirit) in a form of prayer, open to, listening for, welcoming whatever connection or revelation waits for you.

You could, for example, enlist the aid of a child in your life to tell the story of a visit to an elderly or shut-in member of your church. Perhaps that child could create and present a handmade gift. Use your camera to capture each scene of the story. Or perhaps you could show the parallels between the loneliness a child feels (alone at the playground), the loneliness the shut-in feels (abandoned in a nursing home), and how they find and comfort each other, sharing the gift of presence. Your story doesn't need to be a story that actually happened, just a story that flows from your contemplative vision. No matter whether it happened or not, the story will be *true*.

You can also use your photos to illustrate an already existing story. Do you have a favorite Bible story, fable, or children's book? Could you, with photos, illustrate that story or a portion of that story? Could stuffed animals stand in for the story's characters? How about dolls? (Barbie and Ken, I have found, make a passable Eve and Adam.)

I have done this using a poem I wrote about Adam naming the animals. I present the poem on the next page, along with a few of its accompanying photos. I had written the poem long before I decided to illustrate it, so my first step was to look around the house for items to represent *Adam* and *God*, my two main characters. I have an articulated, wire figure of a man (an artist's reference to use when drawing people) and knew he would serve well as my *Adam*. Finding *God* was more challenging; I did not want *God* to appear as another human, so I looked for something more symbolic, more abstract. I own a transparent glass sphere (think "crystal ball") that I use to take creative photos (pictures taken through the sphere yield fascinating, otherworldly images); this, I decided, would take the role of *God*.

With my two leads cast, I needed a few animals for *Adam* to name. Ah, yes—our Christmas nativity. I headed to the storage closet in the garage, delighted to find the Nativity set, in its labeled box, right in front of the stack of Christmas boxes. (We get a gold star for being organized.) I selected a cow, a goat, and a sheep. Now where shall I stage this? I settled on a minimalist set, my light box with a blue background, set up on our card table. Here is the final poem, with two of the eight photos I took to illustrate it:

God Stopped By
God stops by
while Adam names the animals.

A white sheep steps forward:
"Julian," said Adam.

A young goat:
"Carla."

A fawn:
"Samantha."

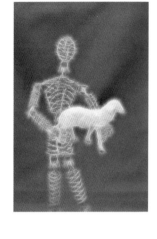

God smiles and shakes God's head.
"No, Adam, that's not it.
Give them *generic* names.
Julian is a *sheep*.
Carla is a *goat*.
Samantha is a *fawn*.
Understand?"

"I think so," Adam says.

Something reptilian slithers at their feet.
"Snake?" Adam asks.

"That's it."
God pauses.
"The problem with personal names?
You become attached,
then they break your heart."

"But you gave *me*
        a personal name."

"Yes."

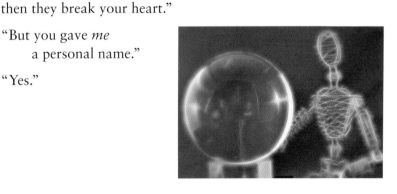

For Reflection:

1. Photographers are storytellers. Mindful, contemplative photographers are mindful, contemplative storytellers. To what extent have you been aware of your dual role as both photographer and storyteller?

2. Consider your favorite photos from the last year or so. What two or three most significant stories do these photos tell?

3. What story would you *like* your photos to tell?

CHAPTER 17

SELF-PORTRAIT

For we are God's handiwork.

—*Ephesians 2:10* NIV

Beyond the Selfie

Ah, the ubiquitous selfie. People have taken pictures of themselves since the invention of the camera, but the widespread use of smartphones with their integrated cameras have made selfies the art form of the twenty-first century. According to a poll conducted for Samsung, selfies make up 30 percent of the pictures taken by eighteen- to twenty-four-year-olds.[1] Let that sink in. Nearly a third of the pictures this group takes are *of themselves*. Of all the amazing things in the world to photograph, I'm going to take pictures of *me*? This is why I often refer to selfies (uncharitably, I admit) as "narcies."

Throughout history, however, the self-portrait has been viewed as a legitimate, desirable art form. The painted, sculpted, drawn, or photographed self-portrait has typically been a carefully considered, thoughtfully crafted, and painstakingly rendered work of art. Rembrandt, Kahlo, Picasso, Warhol, van Gogh, de Vinci, Le Brun, Leibovitz, Mapplethorpe—these are just a few of the world's great artists who created striking, original self-portraits. Now it's your turn.

In terms of your unique contemplative vision and your quest for engaged, thoughtful, meditative photographs, what might your self-portrait look like? What could you say with your self-portrait? Where will you take it? How will you make it original, creative, unique?

---

1. Melanie Hall, "Family Albums Fade as the Young put Only Themselves in Picture," *Telegraph*, June 13, 2013.

Here I present two self-portraits that I have taken over the last few years, along with a bit of commentary on each.

The first is an image I took at the Denver Botanic Garden's gift shop as I explored (with my camera) a display of art-glass vases and bowls. I like this image for several reasons: it shows me engaged in photography, my passion; I took it through layers of glass, which gives a surrealistic, blurred, mystical feeling to the image; the photo works well in black and white; I'm there . . . or am I?—there's a bit of mystery to this image.

 My second example I took at Walt Disney World on the balcony of our resort room. I captured my shadow and the shadow of the railing as they fell across the balcony wall in the light of the setting sun. My arm is up because I'm holding the camera, but at first glance, it could be just a silhouette of someone shielding their eyes from the sun, peering into the distance, or possibly saluting. What pleases me

about this picture? I like its warmth, the parallel shadows of my arm and the balcony railing, and the unique approach to creating a self-portrait using only a shadow.

None of these images are conventional self-portraits (nor the standard selfie). What do these three pictures say about me? My versions of self-portraiture show me obliquely, offering hints as to my identity. I avoid putting my face in your face. I wonder, as I review these, if that reflects some deeper need to conceal who I am?

Creative Self-Portraits

You can easily take a self-portrait by photographing yourself in a mirror. If your camera has a live display—meaning the screen on the back of the camera can be used to frame a picture without having to look through the view-finder—then you can position the camera anywhere, not just in front of your face. (You can do the same thing using your smartphone.) Experiment with taking shots into the mirror—lower, higher, to one side or the other. Turn around and take a few with your back to the camera. Do you have a handheld mirror? Try taking a picture of yourself in one mirror, reflected in the other mirror. Experiment, too, with lighting: take some shots with natural light (if you have a window in your bathroom), others with your bathroom lights, perhaps others with light coming in from a hallway or bedroom.

Place your camera on a tripod and, if your camera has the capability, use the delayed shutter release or a remote shutter release to take pictures. This allows you to pose yourself however you wish in whatever setting you wish. Be creative and keep experimenting. For example, use the tripod to take your picture through the wavy glass of a shower door or through a sheer fabric like a thin scarf of a sheer curtain panel. Play around with a hat, or hide your face in your hands, or peek out around a wall so only one side of your face shows. Express your quirky personality. Play. Remember, you don't need to share any of these photos if you don't wish to.

Take a series of photos which, when sequenced, slowly reveal who you are. Shoot piecemeal . . . a foot, a lower leg, a thigh, your torso, an arm, a hand, your neck, your face and head. Challenge what we normally think of as a portrait (as I did in my examples above). Who says viewing your face is the only way to know you? Aren't you also your neck? Your ear? Your toes? Your knees?

Show your interests in your photos. Do you play the piano? Take photos of your hands on the keyboard. Do you have a dog or cat? Take photos of yourself nose to nose with your pet. Do you cook or garden? Close in on your hands slicing a tomato or harvesting some fresh herbs. Are you in love? Ask your spouse or partner to place a hand on the side of your face; take a close-up picture of that tender interaction.

In short, a contemplative approach to self-portraits will be thoughtful and caring. Respect yourself; honor yourself; love yourself; reveal yourself. Through the lens of your camera, see yourself as God sees you—beautiful, delightful, precious, worthy.

Do take time, once you've experimented with this invitation, to ask what you learn about yourself from your self-portraits. What might a stranger conclude when viewing your self-portraits?

For Reflection:

1. How often have you taken pictures of yourself (selfie or otherwise)? Why have you taken these pictures? What do they reveal about you?

2. After responding to this invitation and reviewing the results, what have you discovered about yourself?

3. The practice of contemplative self-portraiture can easily become the practice of holy self-acceptance and/or sacred self-revelation. To what extent is this true for you?

CHAPTER 18

VISIO DIVINA

Even the simplest thing is as important as the things we consider important. I consider a fallen leaf as important as the Grand Canyon. It's all important; it's all connected. One couldn't be without the other.[1]

—*Ruth Bernhard*

Sacred Seeing

In chapter 1, when speaking of spiritual practices, I mentioned the practice of *lectio divina*, "sacred/divine reading," an ancient method of reading and meditating on scripture. I recommend a similar approach to using photographs (or other works of art) for meditation, called *visio divina*. *Visio divina*, like *lectio divina*, is a way of listening for that still, small voice of God within. Instead of beginning with a passage of scripture, however, you start with something visual, like a painting, a sculpture, or a photograph. *Visio divina* is this chapter's invitation.

To start, select an image from your growing library of contemplative photos, something you feel drawn to, intrigued by. Or, if you like, choose one of the images found on the next page.

Prepare for *visio divina* by sitting quietly, stilling your mind and coming into the moment. Pray for the Holy Spirit to guide you as you engage the image. The four steps of *visio divina* are based on those for *lectio divina*.

Step One: Observe

Be with the image. What, literally, is pictured? Why did you select this image? What attracts you to this image? What

---

1. D. D. Conrad, "Ruth Bernhard," *Camera & Darkroom* (May 1994): 31.

resonates with you? Observe color, texture, shape, contrast, etc. Don't analyze or interpret, just be present. Sit before the image. Let both it and you simply *be*.

Step Two: Listen

Now go deeper. Listen first to what rises within you: What thoughts do you have about the image? What feelings? Memories? Associations? Acknowledge and welcome these. Then ask,

"What might God be saying to me through this image? What might God be asking of me? Wishing for me? Listen for a word of challenge, comfort, wisdom, revelation, hope . . . just listen.

Step Three: Respond

In this step, the one most like traditional prayer, talk to God. Respond to what you heard God say in Step Two. Is there an answer to give? Thanks to express? A question to ask? Praise to offer? This can be a dialogue: you respond, then listen again, then respond, then listen . . .

Step Four: Rest

Conclude with a time of silence and contemplation. Just rest in God's presence. Enjoy God's companionship. Let both mind and body unbend, unfold. God holds you with complete and utter acceptance, and there is nothing for you to do or say. Breathe. Rest.

Visio Divina beyond Photography

You can practice *visio divina* with other forms of art, as mentioned above. You might also employ it when viewing magnificent landscapes (mountains, the ocean, rolling hills) or other scenic wonders (sunrises, sunsets, approaching thunderstorms)—whatever spurs feelings of awe, mystery, or wonder. *Observe. Listen. Respond. Rest.*

I engage with *visio divina* on my solo trips (often to take photos) to the Denver Art Museum and the Denver Museum of Science and Art. Magnificent sculptures and paintings from centuries past draw me in; through them, God speaks. Displays of gemstones, fossils, and world wildlife habitats engage my imagination; meditating with them, I connect with myself, creation, and the divine. Let *visio divina* expand your contemplative vision; savor what you discover.

For Reflection:

1. Toward what types of photos (or other artwork) do you gravitate for *visio divina*?

2. After engaging with an image or two using *visio divina*, describe the experience. What have you learned? How are you different?

3. Think back over your life experiences with great works of art or stunning natural vistas. How have these impacted you? Changed you? Inspired you?

CHAPTER 19

REFLECTION AND REFRACTION

For now we see in a mirror, dimly, but then we will see face to face.

—*1 Corinthians 13:12* NRSV

Divine Distortion

There is no such thing as an objective photograph. Every photograph offers commentary, the photographer's interpretation of the object, person, or event being photographed. You can take a picture mindlessly, but you can *not* take a picture without using your internal lenses and filters, which are every bit as real and influential as camera lenses and filters. Thank about it: every photograph leaves out much more than it includes, and whether consciously or not, you've decided what will be included and what will be left out. The "straight-forward, unbiased" photograph is a myth, a delusion.

It's no different than telling a favorite family story. You include the details that mean the most to you, that enhance the humor or poignancy of the story, that reveal the impact the event had in your life. Ask another family member to relate the same story, and it sounds very different. Every story is a twist on the same event . . . and none is truly objective. It's not unlike the four Gospels—the same basic story of Jesus, but remembered in diverse ways by different people, told with varying intent.

Journalism functions in the same way: the same event covered by the *Washington Post* will have a different spin than if covered by the *Wall Street Journal*. The one we think is most objective will be the one that best fits our own prejudices and assumptions. Every story has a viewpoint.

I don't view this as a bad thing, but I believe it *is* something to be acknowledged and owned. Your photos are *your* interpretation of the world, an expression of *your* contemplative vision. As I asserted in chapter 16, your photos tell your story, unique to you; this is as it should be.

You can enhance and intensify your unique viewpoint by skewing it, by intentionally putting between the viewfinder and your subject other surfaces and "obstacles" that change or modify the captured image. Special lenses dramatically alter what the camera sees, like fish-eye lenses or wide-angle lenses. Filters that attach to your camera lens can provide a variety of modifying effects, like removing specific colors, reducing reflection, and adding starbursts.

You can, however, easily (and inexpensively) achieve your own interesting effects through *reflection* and *refraction,* using objects within reach. In the context of contemplative photography, I call this *divine distortion.* Let's look at each of these individually.

Reflection

Reflective surfaces surround you. Mirrors are the most obvious . . . mirrors in your bathroom, your bedroom, your entry. There are also mirrors on your car . . . at least three. You may carry a mirror in your purse or store one in the garage for seeing under or around items under the hood. Almost any glassy or polished surface can also serve as a mirror: the exterior of your car, the glass covering a framed picture, the glass doors on your fireplace, the chrome exterior of your toaster, the glass door of your oven or microwave, a highly polished floor. Windows also reflect—windows of houses, storefronts, vehicles—as does the surface of water—lakes, streams, puddles, fountains, drops of dew.

Viewing objects or people within reflective surfaces offers many opportunities for creative photography. I refer you back to the picture of the classic New York City hotel reflected in the shiny glass windows of the skyscraper (p. 74); we see the old through the lens of the new. Had I turned and taken a head-on picture of the front of the hotel, it might have been a nice photo, but not nearly as intriguing.

Here is a stained-glass window reflected in the highly polished stone floor of a Chicago cathedral.

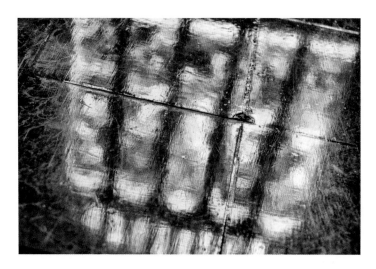

In New York City, I captured this image of a fruit stand reflected in the top of a shiny, black, marble wall. Who would have expected a solid black surface to make the perfect mirror?

Photographing in reflective surfaces often transforms an average (but still photo-worthy) subject into something unexpected and intriguing. I have taken photos of buildings and flowers reflected in puddles, people reflected in storefront windows, clouds reflected in high-rise towers, trees reflected in the frozen surface of ponds, cityscapes reflected and framed in the side mirrors of cars and trucks.

There is something inherently mysterious about reflections. Reflections remind us that there's another side to every viewpoint. Reflections reverse our perspective. When we view ourselves in a mirror, we're actually viewing ourselves flipped; left becomes right and right becomes left. Is this how people see us? No, it's not—we can't actually see how we look to others when viewing ourselves in a mirror. Reflected images encourage us to ask: What's real here and what's not? What's to be trusted and what's not? These are excellent questions for contemplative vision.

So this chapter's first invitation is take photos of the reflections of things. See what you find in mirrors, windows, ponds, and other reflective surfaces. Discover how your perspective changes when seeing things "second-hand," not straight on.

Refraction

Refraction involves the bending of light, the changing of its direction. A prism, for example, is a solid, transparent body that disperses light into the separate colors of the spectrum. The light entering a prism bends (refracts) and emerges as a rainbow. As a kid, you likely were fascinated by the seeming magic of prisms. Now, as a contemplative photographer, you can explore the magic of refraction and what it can do for your photos.

I shared one example of refraction in the photo of my friend's glass globe in his home in San Francisco (p. 38). The glass ball I used to represent God when illustrating the story of Adam naming the animals (p. 98) creates striking images when placed between the camera and your subject. Here, for example, is a picture I took with a wooden model of a lighthouse viewed through the ball. I flipped the image over so that the refracted lighthouse is right side up.

The photo below is a glass Christmas ornament hanging from the roof in a greenhouse at the Denver Botanic Gardens. Refracted in the ball of the ornament are the supports for the glass roof.

Where else do you find refracted light? Look around your home for objects that "bend" and "break" light. Check out glass vases, bottles, jars, and cookware. Clear or translucent plastic items will also work. Various colors of glass (still clear enough to see through) add an additional dimension to refraction photos. Spend time taking photographs with and through these items. This is the second of your invitations in this chapter.

And So On

Be open to other, unexpected ways to see familiar scenes when something intervenes between your camera lens and your subject. Shooting through glass, as seen here in a photo from the Nashville airport looking out onto the rainy tarmac, is another option. You can't see it when this photo is reproduced at this size, but if enlarged, every water drop on the window contains a tiny image of the waiting plane.

It's all about you and your contemplative vision, searching for and embracing the unexpected, the usual seen unusually, the ordinary transmuted into the extraordinary. *Be open and be amazed.*

For Reflection:

1. What opportunities have you found to take reflection photos? What new things have you seen, thought, and felt through this invitation?

2. What opportunities have you found to take refraction photos? What new things have you seen, thought, and felt through this invitation?

3. In terms of your own walk with God, where do you see God "reflected" or "refracted" in the world around you? In the people around you? In yourself?

CHAPTER 20

BLACK AND WHITE

There is a visceral connection between a viewer and a black-and-white photograph that does not exist with color photography.[1]

—Chris Bucher

When Less Is More

Meditation means reduction. In meditation, less leads to more, to something greater. The "less" of silence, stillness, and open receptivity leads to insight, connection, awareness, and raw experience, a direct knowing beneath and beyond words.

In a similar way, meditative photography aims to reduce input and distraction to make space for creativity and inspiration. Reduction in photography means narrowing the focus, stripping away the nonessential, seeing only what leads, moves, calls to us. It can mean clearing out the space around you—at home or out in the field—physically, mentally, emotionally, and visually.

We've seen that this can be done by moving in closer to our subject. It can be done by backing off as well, letting many elements merge into a single, larger element, as when individual people become a crowd, or trees a forest. We also do it by focusing on particular elements, like color or pattern, texture or form. Art speaks most powerfully when speaking most simply. (God speaks powerfully because God speaks simply.)

You can also simplify, narrow, and focus with black-and-white photography. That's not to say all great black-and-white photos are simple and uncluttered, but that capturing an image without color (or removing the color after the photo has been taken) reduces the amount of visual input and thus, may, given

---

1. Chris Bucher, *Black and White Digital Photography Photo Workshop* (Indianapolis: Wiley Publishing, 2011), 5.

the subject, enable us to see the subject in new ways. As photographer Chris Bucher tells us, "Just when you think you've seen something a million times, you see it in black and white. Suddenly, it is new and fresh, or old and nostalgic, or gritty, or has a cool, clean contemporary look that is totally surprising."[2] Black-and-white photography offers the potential to reveal the "hidden soul" (the depth, the beauty, the uniqueness) of many subjects.

Contemplative vision sees beyond the normal, sees what conventional vision does not, sees through the surface into the divine heart of objects, landscapes, people. Black-and-white photography can facilitate this.

Let's revisit the dahlia I shared in chapter 3. Here you see that photo again, plus a color version very close to the original. Both started with the same photo. For the color version, I slightly enhanced the color, strengthened the sharpness/detail, and added the light vignette. For the black-and-white version, I softened the image overall, slightly boosted contrast, and added the dark vignette. What other differences do you observe between them? What differences do you experience in terms of thoughts and feelings, connections and meaning?

I find both images to be beautiful and satisfying—and calming. My experience of the first, the color image, feels more technical, botanical, analytical. I see an amazing flower, with striking form, detail, color. I note the pastel shades of pink, purple, and pale green, all contrasting with the white. Would

---

2. Bucher, *Black and White Digital Photography*, 21.

I consider printing and hanging this? I would . . . until I compare it to the black-and-white version, which I like even more. I had to choose which of these images to include in chapter 3; I went with the black-and-white version because I find it to be the more engaging, the more potent. It's hard to put into words, but I "feel" the black-and-white version in a different way; my experience is that of softness, comfort, invitation, ease. While both versions feel peaceful, the black-and-white version reaches deeper; it's meditative, dreamlike, even holy. I experience wonder with both, but "being with" the black-and-white image (in a *visio divina* sort of way) verges on worship.

And now you may be thinking, "Umm . . . good heavens, you see an awful lot in that picture." Well, I do, and perhaps you do too . . . and perhaps not. That's okay. The point remains—and becomes one for you to explore—that the experience of black-and-white photography can result in the creation of very different, delightfully surprising images. And that's your invitation: create black-and-white images of objects, people, and landscapes that you would normally photograph in color.

Some Suggestions

Your camera or phone may allow you to take photos in black-and-white. If not, the most basic of photo-manipulation programs will convert photos for you. Most programs will also give you choices for black-and-white conversion, which simulate the use of different filters and processing options (analogous to what film developers do in their labs). Experiment with taking pictures in black and white as well as converting color images to black and white and see what results you get.

Think "monochromatic," not just "black and white." In other words, what I've been saying about black-and-white images also applies to monochromatic images that you process using a single color other than black. Many old photographs were taken using black and white film (which was all there was early on) and then printed in shades of brown or other muted colors (depending on the process). Sepia-toned photos are common, and you can create that effect in photo-processing programs (and, in fact, some cameras offer a sepia setting to use as you take your pictures). Do you have old black-and-white family photos that have yellowed with age? You can experiment with coloring your black-and-white photos to look like these vintage photos. Here, for example, is a sepia-toned photo of a seed pod. The photo is a new one but treated to look old.

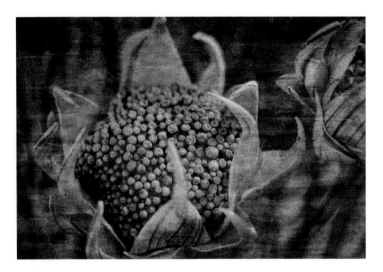

Look for monochromatic subjects, that is, subjects that are, in their natural state, primarily a single color or shades of a single color. You may not need to convert these photos to black-and-white to get the impact of a black-and-white photo.

In a black-and-white photograph, more emphasis naturally falls on line, shape, and shadow. In choosing potential subjects, note how these three elements play off each other. Try to engage that play.

Both textures and patterns often appear more compelling in black-and-white photos. Look for opportunities to capture both, as I've done in the picture at the top of the page.

Look for a strong contrast in your black-and-white subjects, in other words, try to capture pictures that contain very light to very dark tones, with lots of shades of gray in between. Look again at  the picture of the bricks above, noting how there are areas of nearly pure white (on the mortar) to black (the shadows under the mortar), as well as many shades of gray spreading over the bricks. The greater this range of contrast, the more visual interest in the photo.

Black-and-white photos tend to make kinder portraits, so include family members and friends as potential subjects. Pay special attention to people's eyes, as I did in this photo of our friend Kevin.

In general, let your contemplative vision guide you . . . and keep experimenting to see what you end up with. There are photographers so enamored by black-and-white photography that this becomes their sole focus. I find an emotional intensity in black-and-white photography that I find less often in color photography. Why might this  be? I haven't figured it out, yet, but I know it has something to do with clarity and focus and simplicity.

For Reflection:

1. When in your photography have you experienced the truth of "less is more"?

2. To what extent do black-and-white photos appeal to you? Explain.

3. After experimenting with black-and-white photography and reviewing your results, which images speak most powerfully to you? Why?

CHAPTER 21

ABSTRACTION

Open your mind. See a chair, and you'll photograph a chair. But view it as a collection of visual ingredients, and you can craft an innovate shot.[1]

—Weldon Owen

It Is What It Is

I now extend to you my favorite of the dozen invitations: I invite you to create images without identifiable content, simply capturing pure form, color, movement, or texture. Create images that leave your viewers wondering, "What *is* it?" Create *abstract* images.

Abstract art attempts to communicate without clearly representing the object or idea being depicted in the artwork. Sculptors or painters may draw their abstract ideas purely from imagination, without any objective reference to concrete items in the world, but a photographer takes pictures of *things*, things that actually exist, and so photographic abstract images start with *real* objects, not imagined. The real objects in abstract photography, however, are rendered in such a way that the pattern, texture, form, color of the subjects become the new subject of the photos, not the subject itself.

I've shared a number of abstract photos throughout the book, including the fan (p. 39), the Christmas ornament (p. 59), the Chicago high-rise (p. 72), and the tea ball (p. 88). Some viewers may correctly identify these original subjects, but most won't, or at least most will struggle. Abstraction comes in degrees, from possibly recognizable to completely obscure. What abstract images share is an intent to set aside the overall

---

1. Weldon Owen, *The Complete Photo Manual* (Palm Coast, FL: Popular Photography, 2012), #127.

subject of the photos to focus on more essential, basic elements of that subject. As the opening quote from Weldon Owen might suggest, don't photograph the chair, photograph a curve, a texture, a pattern, an insight, a feeling, a revealing bit of the chair. Let that bit become the subject. We know chairs; what we don't know is the beauty and wonder hidden in chairs, waiting to be discovered and shared.

Most people don't realize (but contemplative photographers like you, do) that we see *bits and pieces* of a thing more often than the *whole* thing. This is one reason that casual photographers are often disappointed in what they capture with their cameras. Janelle, for example, sees a fascinating, strangely contorted tree while walking in a local park. Because of how Janelle's eye and brain process visual input, she sees the tree, but *not* all the other trees, the surrounding buildings, the undergrowth, the picnickers. If at this moment someone drew this to Janelle's attention, she would say, "Oh, yes, of course, all that is there too," but no one does. Instead, Janelle raises her phone and takes a picture of what she perceives is the tree. But when Janelle previews the shot on the back of her phone, she sees, to her dismay, that the tree is a rather dismal, minor figure in the photo. It's lost in the background of other trees or buildings. Our eyes and minds frame, filter, recompose what we see all the time, but the camera does not. The camera will capture *everything* in front of its lens. Our brains reconstruct what we see based on our interests, experiences, and desires, but not so the camera. With cameras, we may experience a disconnect between our perception and what we capture in a photo. How often do you look at a photo you've taken and say, either, "Yes, that's exactly what I saw" or, conversely, like Janelle, "Well, that wasn't it at all"?

We see more abstractly than we realize. As I sit at my computer typing, I look up and see a shallow, hand-crafted, wooden bowl that hangs on the wall in front of me. It's a work of art, painted with a simple bird and other lines, swirls, and squiggles. When I look at it, I see the bird's beak, which is orange. I see four metal rivets, but only one at a time, too far away from each to take them all in at once; I need to look at each individually. There are four patches of muted color. And the work includes a signature, which I can't read, but it starts with *R* and ends with *S*. I do not see all of these elements at once. My eyes—both physical and mental—jump from detail to detail. The bowl is the sum of those details. And if that's how we see (just as with Janelle and the tree she liked), then that is how we can photograph. A shot of a rivet, or the bird's beak, or a swirl or squiggle will, for me, bring to mind the experience of the bowl, because I'm so familiar with it, but for a viewer not familiar with the bowl, those will be abstract bits unrelated to their experience.

Let me illustrate with two photos. Take a minute to look both, then I'll talk more about each. What do *you* see?

The first of these images is the view looking down into a martini glass. The bowl of the glass is green and clear, dotted with air bubbles. The lighter area surrounding the dark dot in the center of the photo is the white, frosted stem of the glass. The second image is of a handheld, battery-powered fan (about 5" in diameter) whose two soft-plastic blades are embedded with tiny LED lights. When the fan is on, the lights in the blades turn on and off randomly, forming ever-changing patterns. I photographed this in the dark, and the long shutter speeds set by the camera captured—and blurred—the spinning lights.

The meaning found in any photo is a combination of the original vision of the photographer *and* the response of the viewer. This becomes even more evident with abstract photos, especially when the viewer has no clue what the subject is. That's one of the things I love most about sharing abstract photos— listening and learning what the viewer sees, which is very often something that never would have occurred to me.

Taking Abstract Photos

My two samples found on the previous page clearly illustrate one thing: You'll find great subjects for abstract photography all over your home. Look "beyond the chair" to the elements of the chair. Look beyond the bowl, the light fixture, the bag of dog food, the toolbox, the lampshade, the pile of unfolded laundry, or the sole of your shoe to the elements found in these. Look to see the abstract possibilities. It's all there in front of you.

Come in close. That's obvious from my samples on the previous page. To extract the elements from the broader subject, fill the frame with just the element of interest. Had I taken the picture of the martini glass from a few inches farther away, it would have been a photo of a martini glass; as it is now, it's a photo of something watery and mysterious. And keep in mind, in a photo-manipulation program, you can crop an image to eliminate the context and keep only the intriguing, mysterious element you wish to retain. Had I taken the photo of the martini glass from too far away, I could have cropped it to look like the image as shown.

You may find, as I have, that abstract photos come as happy accidents. Occasionally, I mean to capture one thing but end up with something even more interesting. Why? Perhaps the camera moved. Perhaps I overlooked a setting and the image is washed out or too dark. Perhaps the camera failed to focus where I'd wanted it to focus, but the blurred result has its own odd appeal. Don't be too quick to delete the photos that look like mistakes; perhaps one or two of them hold abstract appeal.

If you enjoy manipulating images on the computer or your phone, experiment with the sorts of programs discussed in chapter 8. You can create an abstract image from nearly any photo you've taken. I take pictures of some subjects solely to use them to create something abstract. I look for patterns and shapes that I know, from experience, could result in something strange and new. Here's an example, showing the original photo—taken with the intent of playing with it back home on the computer—and the resulting, abstract image.

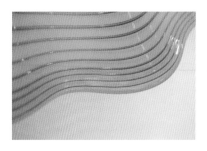 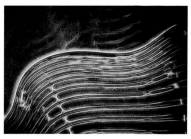

The original image is of the edge of a glass bowl for sale in a museum gift shop. On the right is the image I created on the computer. To me, the new image looks like the wing of some mystical bird . . . or perhaps an angel. It speaks of escape into an imagined world, into *my* imagined world.

And speaking of imagined worlds, release yourself to create the unknown worlds you see with your contemplative vision. Abstract photography is much like writing a fantasy story— you can do whatever you want, create whatever appeals to you, and make it entirely yours, expressing your unique ideas and feelings. Perhaps that's why abstract photography so appeals to me. I enjoy utter freedom to see whatever I want to see.

For Reflection:

1. In the past, how have you related to abstract art? What appeals to you? What does *not* appeal to you?

2. Take a quick look around your home. List here a dozen potential subjects for abstract photos.

3. After experimenting with abstract photography, review your results and ask: What do I like about these images? What do these images say about me? About my relationship with the world around me? About my relationship to God?

CONCLUSION

ON BEING AND SEEING

Alchemy, it is said, changes common metal to gold.
We do that with our cameras,
transforming the ordinary and overlooked
   into images of wonder,
and our everyday hearts
   into receptacles for God.

Summing Up

So what, then, is contemplative vision? Is it a way of seeing? Or is it a way of being? It is both. It is a way of being that will, for the photographer, result in a way of seeing. It is a way of being and seeing that increasingly manifests in images that reveal the remarkable in the everyday world around us, images that draw the photographer and the viewer closer to the threshold between the physical and the spiritual, between this world and the next, images that lead us into awe and appreciation, silence and insight, intimacy and eternity. One cannot *see* contemplatively without *living*, at least part of the time, contemplatively. You do this now; I suspect you will do this more.

What, then, is contemplative photography? Is it a way of taking pictures? Or is it the state of the photographer when taking those pictures? Does the contemplative, meditative quality reside in the images themselves? Or is it actually in the observer? Does it *become* contemplative photography because the viewer experiences it as such, is engaged, moved, reflects, and turns inward? It can be any or all of these, and it will be different—and always changing—for different photographers and different viewers.

For all of us, both photographers and observers, it's what we, as individuals, bring to our subjects and our final images.

Meditators, contemplatives, mystics, you, me—we are more likely to receive and see contemplative images the more we live into and out of stillness, in-the-moment presence, receptivity, and attentive awareness. And in doing so, we live into and out of our silent, ever-present, welcoming, and attentive God.

For Reflection:

1. What are the most interesting, surprising, and/or challenging lessons you've learned as you've become more intentional about photography as a spiritual practice?

2. If you've been writing in this book, look back through your journaling. What's this journey look like? How have you changed through the process? How has your photography changed through the process?

PART 4

RESOURCES

RECOMMENDED READING

Ang, Tom. *Tao of Photography: Unlock Your Creativity Using the Wisdom of the East.* NY: Amphoto Books, 2000.

Brackenbury, John. *Close Up: Creative Techniques for Successful Macrophotography.* Brighton and Hove, UK: RotoVision, 2004.

Davis, Harold. *Creative Close-ups: Digital Photography Tips & Techniques.* Berkeley, CA: Harold Davis Art & Photography, 2009.

DuBose, Julie. *Effortless Beauty: Photography as an Expression of Eye, Mind and Heart.* Boulder, CO: Miksang Publication, 2013.

Gross, Philippe L., and S. I. Shapiro. *The Tao of Photography: Seeing Beyond Seeing.* Berkeley, CA: Ten Speed Press, 2001.

Hoffman, Torsten Andreas. *Photography as Meditation: Tap into the Source of Your Creativity.* Santa Barbara, CA: Rocky Nook, 2014.

Karr, Andy, and Michael Wood. *The Practice of Contemplative Photography: Seeing the World with Fresh Eyes.* Boston and London: Shambhala, 2011.

Martin, Giles, and Ronan Laoëc. Tr. by Lenora Ammon. *Macrophotography: Learning from a Master.* NY: Abrams, 2003.

Milburn, Ken. *Digital Abstract and Macro Photography.* Boston: Thomson, 2005.

Orwig, Chris. *Visual Poetry: A Creative Guide for Making Engaging Digital Photographs.* Berkeley, CA: New Riders, 2010.

Patterson, Freeman. *Photography and the Art of Seeing: A Visual Perception Workshop for Film and Digital Photography.* Toronto: Key Porter Books, 2004.

Peterson, Bryan. *Learning to See Creatively: Design, Color and Composition in Photography* (rev. ed.). New York: Amphoto Books, 2003.

———. *Understanding Close-Up Photography: Creative Close Encounters with or without a Macro Lens.* New York: Amphoto Books, 2009.

Phillips, Jan. *God Is at Eye Level: Photography as Healing Art.* Wheaton, IL: Quest Books, 2000.

Shaw, John. *Closeups in Nature: The Photographer's Guide to Techniques in the Field.* New York: Amphoto Books, 1987.

Tharp, Brenda, and Jed Manwaring. *Extraordinary Everyday Photography: Awaken Your Vision to Create Stunning Images Wherever You Are.* New York: Amphoto, 2012.

Zehr, Howard. *The Little Book of Contemplative Photography: Seeing with Wisdom, Respect, and Humility.* Intercourse, PA: Good Books, 2005.

Software and Apps

Note: The following list, while extensive, is far from exhaustive. Search online to discover additional options. Keep in mind that websites and online addresses frequently change; if the addresses below do not work, try searching by software title or website name instead.

Photo-Manipulation Programs:

Note: Some of the following programs offer free trial periods. Others offer free, slimmed-down versions but charge for the full version. The program GIMP is a full-featured and completely free program—a good place to start.

- Adobe Lightroom: *https://www.adobe.com/products/photoshop -lightroom.html*
- Adobe Photoshop: *https://www.adobe.com/products/photoshop.html*
- Adobe Photoshop Elements: *https://www.adobe.com/products /photoshop-elements.html*
- Corel PaintShop: *https://www.paintshoppro.com/en/*
- CyberLink PhotoDirector: *https://www.cyberlink.com/products /photodirector-ultra/features_en_US.html*
- FotoWorks XL: *http://www.fotoworks-xl.com/photo-editing-software. shtml*
- GIMP (free, open-source program): *https://www.gimp.org*
- Microsoft Photos (for Windows): *https://www.microsoft.com/en-us/p /microsoft-photos/9wzdncrfjbh4?activetab=pivot%3aoverviewtab*
- NCH Software PhotoPad: *https://www.nchsoftware.com/photoeditor /index.html*
- On1 Photo Raw: *https://www.on1.com/products/photo-raw/*
- Photo Reactor: *https://mediachance.com/reactor/index.html*
- Photos (for Mac): *https://support.apple.com/en-us/ht206186*
- Skylum Luminar: *https://skylum.com*
- Topaz Studio: *https://topazlabs.com/studio/*

Plug-ins for Existing Programs:

- Alien Skin Software: *https://www.alienskin.com/*
- AlphaPlugins: *https://www.alphaplugins.com/common/default.php ?menu=purchase*
- Andromeda Software: *http://andromeda.com/wordpress/individual -products*
- Auto FX Software: *http://www.autofx.com/*
- Digital Anarchy: *https://digitalanarchy.com/index.html*
- Digital Film Tools: *http://www.digitalfilmtools.com/*

- Flaming Pear Software: *http://www.flamingpear.com/index.html*
- MediaChance: *https://www.mediachance.com/plugins/index.html*
- Mister Retro: *https://www.misterretro.com/filters*
- On1 Software: *https://www.on1.com/products/effects10/*
- Topaz Labs: *https://topazlabs.com/shop*

Stand-Alone Programs with Specific Functions:

- Dynamic Auto Painter: *https://www.mediachance.com/dap/*
- Dynamic Photo HDR: *https://www.mediachance.com/hdri/index.html*
- Photo-Blend 3D: *https://www.mediachance.com/photoblend/index.html*
- Quick HDR: *https://www.mediachance.com/quickhdr/index.html*

Software for iPhones:

- Adobe Photoshop Express: *https://itunes.apple.com/us/app/adobe -photoshop-express/id331975235?mt=8*
- Afterlight: *https://itunes.apple.com/us/app/afterlight-2/id1293122457 ?mt=8*
- Camera+: *https://itunes.apple.com/us/app/camera/id329670577?mt=8*
- Enlight: *https://itunes.apple.com/us/app/enlight/id930026670?mt=8*
- Mextures: *https://itunes.apple.com/us/app/mextures/id650415564?mt=8*
- Polarr: *https://itunes.apple.com/us/app/polarr-photo-editor/id988173374 ?mt=8*
- ProCamera: *https://itunes.apple.com/us/app/procamera/id694647259 ?mt=8*
- Snapseed: *https://snapseed.en.softonic.com/iphone*
- Touch Retouch: *https://itunes.apple.com/us/app/touchretouch/id 373311252?mt=8*

Software for Android Phones:

- Adobe Photoshop Express: *https://play.google.com/store/apps/details ?id=com.adobe.psmobile&hl=en_US*
- AirBrush: *https://play.google.com/store/apps/details?id=com.magicv. airbrush*
- Aviary: *https://play.google.com/store/apps/details?id=com.aviary. android.feather*
- Cymera: *https://play.google.com/store/apps/details?id=com.cyworld. camera*
- Open Camera: *https://play.google.com/store/apps/details?id=net.source forge.opencamera*

- PhotoDirector: *https://play.google.com/store/apps/details?id=com.cyberlink.photodirector*
- Photo Lab: *https://play.google.com/store/apps/details?id=vsin.t16_funny_photo*
- PicsArt Photo Studio: *https://play.google.com/store/apps/details?id=com.picsart.studio*
- Pixlr: *https://play.google.com/store/apps/details?id=com.pixlr.express*
- Snapseed: *https://play.google.com/store/apps/details?id=com.niksoftware.snapseed*

Contemplative Photography Websites:

Note: Find inspiration and resources at the following sites and blogs. There are many more helpful sites on the web than I have listed here; search for *Meditation and Photography, Zen Photography, Contemplative Photography*, and so on, and see what you discover.

- Contemplative Photography: *http://woodenhue.blogspot.com/*
- 5 Ultimate Reasons Why Photography Is Meditation: *http://121clicks.com/tutorials/5-ultimate-reasons-why-photography-is-meditation*
- Lion's Roar: *https://www.lionsroar.com/how-to-practice-contemplative-photography/*
- Miksang Contemplative Photography: *https://www.miksang.com/*
- Mindfulness in Photography: *http://truecenterpublishing.com/photopsy/mindfulness.htm*
- National Geographic: The Art of Mindful Photography: *https://www.nationalgeographic.com/travel/intelligent-travel/2014/06/06/mindful-photography-jonathan-foust/*
- Seeing Fresh: The Practice of Contemplative Photography: *http://seeingfresh.com/*
- The 7 Ways of Zen Landscape Photography: *https://fstoppers.com/fine-art/7-ways-zen-landscape-photography-116392*
- The 60-Second Sabbath: *http://www.the60secondsabbath.com/*
- Zen: Musings on the Meditative Act of Photography: *https://www.thephoblographer.com/2017/03/24/the-meditative-act-of-photography/*